Freud Explained

Volumes in the Series:

Mourning Freud
by Madelon Sprengnether

Does the Internet Have an Unconscious?: Slavoj Žižek and Digital Culture
by Clint Burnham

In the Event of Laughter: Psychoanalysis, Literature and Comedy
by Alfie Bown

On Dangerous Ground: Freud's Visual Cultures of the Unconscious
by Diane O'Donoghue

For Want of Ambiguity: Order and Chaos in Art, Psychoanalysis, and Neuroscience
by Ludovica Lumer and Lois Oppenheim

Life Itself Is an Art: The Life and Work of Erich Fromm
by Rainer Funk

Born After: Reckoning with the German Past
by Angelika Bammer

Critical Theory between Klein and Lacan: A Dialogue
by Amy Allen and Mari Ruti

Transferences: The Aesthetics and Poetics of the Therapeutic Relationship
by Maren Scheurer

At the Risk of Thinking: An Intellectual Biography of Julia Kristeva
by Alice Jardine, edited by Mari Ruti

The Writing Cure
by Emma Lieber

The Analyst's Desire: The Ethical Foundation of Clinical Practice
by Mitchell Wilson

Our Two-Track Minds: Rehabilitating Freud on Culture
by Robert A. Paul

Norman N. Holland: The Dean of American Psychoanalytic Literary Critics
by Jeffrey Berman

Psychological Roots of the Climate Crisis: Neoliberal Exceptionalism and the Culture of Uncare
by Sally Weintrobe

Circumcision on the Couch: The Cultural, Psychological and Gendered Dimensions of the World's Oldest Surgery
by Jordan Osserman

The Racist Fantasy: Unconscious Roots of Hatred
by Todd McGowan

Antisemitism and Racism: Ethical Challenges for Psychoanalysis
by Stephen Frosh

The Ethics of Immediacy: Dangerous Experience in Freud, Woolf, and Merleau-Ponty
by Jeffrey McCurry

Analyzed by Lacan: A Personal Account
by Betty Milan

Visual Culture in Freud's Vienna
by Mary Bergstein

Genius after Psychoanalysis
by K. Daniel Cho

Psychoanalysis and the Patriarchal Tradition: Augustine to Milton
by Peter L. Rudnytsky

Film Adaptation and the Real: Subjectivity and Cinematic Mediation
by Hee-Seung Irene Lee

Freud Explained: Psychoanalysis from Vienna to Exile
by Stephen Frosh

PSYCHOANALYTIC HORIZONS

Psychoanalysis is unique in being at once a theory and a therapy, a method of critical thinking and a form of clinical practice. Now in its second century, this fusion of science and humanism derived from Freud has outlived all predictions of its demise. **Psychoanalytic Horizons** evokes the idea of a convergence between realms as well as the outer limits of a vision. Books in the series test disciplinary boundaries and will appeal to scholars and therapists who are passionate not only about the theory of literature, culture, media, and philosophy but also, above all, about the real life of ideas in the world.

Freud Explained

Psychoanalysis from Vienna to Exile

Stephen Frosh

BLOOMSBURY ACADEMIC
NEW YORK • LONDON • OXFORD • NEW DELHI • SYDNEY

BLOOMSBURY ACADEMIC
Bloomsbury Publishing Inc, 1359 Broadway, New York, NY 10018, USA
Bloomsbury Publishing Plc, 50 Bedford Square, London, WC1B 3DP, UK
Bloomsbury Publishing Ireland, 29 Earlsfort Terrace, Dublin 2, D02 AY28, Ireland

BLOOMSBURY, BLOOMSBURY ACADEMIC and the Diana logo
are trademarks of Bloomsbury Publishing Plc

First published in the United States of America, 2026

Series design by Daniel Benneworth-Gray
Cover image: Sigmund Freud (1856-1939) © Photo 12 / Universal
Images Group / Getty Images

Library of Congress Cataloguing-in-Publication Data

ISBN: HB: 979-8-216-37200-4
PB: 979-8-216-37199-1
ePDF: 979-8-216-37202-8
eBook: 979-8-216-37203-5

Series: Psychoanalytic Horizons

Typeset by Integra Software Services Pvt. Ltd.
Printed and bound in the United States of America

For product safety related questions contact productsafety@bloomsbury.com.

Contents

Preface

Sigmund Freud (1856–1939) was the founder of psychoanalysis and one of the most influential writers of modern times. He invented a way of thinking about people that emphasizes the importance of their inner world of desires and wishes, and he developed a practice of psychotherapy that set the stage for all the "talking cures" with which we are now familiar. In a famous poem commemorating Freud's death, W. H. Auden wrote of him that "he is no more a person / now but a whole climate of opinion," expressing how Freud's ideas have come to be vital aspects of contemporary life.[1] The unconscious, sexual repression, free association, the interpretation of dreams, even "therapeutic culture" all have their place at the center of western society because of Freud. But he was a person too, ambitious, conflicted, amorous, irritable, blind about some things but prophetically insightful about others. In fact, his personality shaped the way psychoanalysis developed, and its texts are full of vignettes from Freud's life—the dreams he had, the jokes he told, and the patients he worked with. Remarkably, psychoanalysis is a discipline built on the dream life of its creator.

This book presents a biographical introduction to Freud and to his major ideas. It describes his life in nineteenth-century Vienna and the patients with whom he worked. It looks at the relationships he formed with his teachers and followers, including his passionate links with men with whom he subsequently fell out. It focuses on how his theories developed in the context of the enormous social and political upheavals of the early twentieth century. These disruptions eventually prompted Freud to move to England as an exile, in order, as he wrote in 1938 to his son Ernst, "to die in freedom."[2]

But why do we need another book about Freud? After all, not only has he been dead for over three-quarters of a century, but his *intellectual* death has been declared many times. Yet he has often been quickly resurrected, as in a famous *Newsweek* cover of 2006 that inserted the word "Not" into the title "Freud is Dead."[3] The passion surrounding the question of whether there is anything worth keeping alive in "Freud"—that is, in his ideas and in the legacy he gave the world, i.e., psychoanalysis—continues to be intense. One contributor to the *Newsweek* article defending Freud complained afterwards that he had been misquoted, and for every defense, there is at least one virulent attack. In addition, there seems to be no end of books about Freud, including a series of biographies ranging from the whimsical and partial, to the deeply scholarly and appreciatively critical. Since 2000, when the Library of Congress opened most of its archives of Freud's documents, there has been at least one major study (by French historian and psychoanalyst Elisabeth Roudinesco) that incorporates much of what is known about Freud, and it is possible to argue that there is not really much left to be said. So why yet another book?

One simple answer is that Freud remains a fascinating character, whose ideas are constantly inviting reconsideration and reevaluation, and whose impact on western culture is so profound that it is always open to review. Each one of us is absorbed to a greater or lesser extent in what has been termed a "psychoanalytic culture," meaning that we tend to understand ourselves and other people through the lens of Freudian ideas. For example, we might acknowledge the limits of our ability to be sure of our desires or wishes, or of the reasons for our behavior. Do I always know why I do certain things, or think certain thoughts, or find myself lost in some fantasy or dream? What are the reasons for a person's inability to stay rational or keep their temper? What explanation could there be for the repetitive way in which some people sabotage themselves just when they seem to be on the verge of a significant achievement? There are clearly many possible answers to these questions. Nevertheless, it is very hard to approach them without some consideration of basic Freudian ideas, such as that we might have unconscious wishes of which, by definition, we are unaware, or only very partially aware; or that we may have unresolved conflicts which spill over into everyday life, or confused recollections or even traumatic memories that are not fully known to us, yet are having an impact on our behavior. This is a way of saying that humans are "reflexive" beings: we use the intellectual tools at our disposal, including some powerful ideas put forward by Freud, to make sense of ourselves and the world.

There is also something about Freud himself. His writings are purportedly scientific and at times philosophical, but he was also an expert in a genre of *personal* writing, in two major senses. One is that he characteristically used the "I" form in his works, so a reader gets a strong sense of Freud's presence in his texts, of his views, of his manner as a presenter of arguments, and of his doubts and uncertainties. This strong feeling of Freud's presence has a kind of uncanny effect: if you read enough of his work, you might feel that you know him as a person. This effect is amplified by the way he drew very directly on his own experience in much of his writing. This was not just his reports of his clinical cases, but also his own dreams and mistakes, and often his memories. Some of these papers are about himself; others use his own situation or vignettes from his life as examples. This means that, rather extraordinarily, this "science" of psychoanalysis is very personal, and the person it originates from and is most replete with is Freud himself. This is why his life is not peripheral to his invention, as he himself might at times have wished. Psychoanalysis is one of the most intimate kinds of knowledge, based on deep exploration of the unconscious life of its patients. But the intimacy does not stop there: it also speaks about the people who use psychoanalysis, those who write about it, and those who consume it as readers and thinkers. Above all, it speaks of Freud himself.

Each new book on Freud is a way of engaging with the world through the lens of psychoanalysis, and with psychoanalysis through the lens of Freud himself. His was also a kind of exemplary life in that it spanned an important period in relatively recent history. This was the period of the end of the European empire and the fantasy of Europe as the high point of human civilization. It included the cataclysmic impact of political and cultural revolution, the First World War and the rise of Nazism. Freud's life and thought were intimately bound up with these great events, and although he spent most of his life in one city—Vienna—the powerful social forces swirling around him had a profound impact on his thought. In many ways, he helped define the new human realities: how passionate irrationalities break through; how sexual hypocrisy damages people; how we need to live lighter and more open lives; how dreams and fantasies dominate us; and how destructiveness seems to be a basic element in life and in society. Understanding Freud is one route into beginning to grasp some of these issues, which remain relevant even today. For example, can we claim that either sex or violence no longer plays any part in our society? Freud's life and work are at one with each other, providing insight into the conditions of modern living.

And finally, many books on Freud are long, for the very good reason that he lived a long life and wrote a great amount, and that much of what he experienced and wrote about is complex and needs careful explanation. This particular book is short and, I hope, easily accessible. It is based on those lengthier works—especially those written by Peter Gay, George Makari, and Elisabeth Roudinesco, as well as on some of my own earlier publications. My aim here is to introduce some of the main elements of Freud's life and work, and to convey once again why—whether right or wrong—the founder of psychoanalysis is not dead in an intellectual or cultural sense.

Stephen Frosh
London, England

1

Childhood: "My Golden Sigi"

It is hard to write about Sigmund Freud's childhood without a crippling sense of responsibility. After all, this is the man who probably did more than anyone to establish the centrality of childhood in development. Of course, he did not do this alone. William Wordsworth's line "The Child is father to the Man" predates Freud's psychoanalytic writings by about 100 years,[1] and plenty of others—the eighteenth-century philosopher Jean-Jacques Rousseau, for instance—had the same idea. Still, Freud was the one who most systematically explained the importance of childhood for settling the character and fortune of each one of us, even if the way he did this was, and remains, controversial.

Freud himself is the most important source for our knowledge of his childhood years. This has both advantages and disadvantages. On the positive side, his willingness to share some of his early memories and to provide the interpretation for them saves a biographer a lot of work. As so many biographies use Freudian ideas to make sense of the life in hand, we can even see this as a shortcut: Freud himself provided the memory and its explanation in a way that, given his expertise, no one can really challenge. On the other hand, not only does this close some doors (how do you argue about the significance of childhood with the founder of psychoanalysis himself?), but also Freud was certainly not immune to the difficulty of remembering accurately, or sometimes at all—a difficulty that plagues all of us. In addition, because he realized that childhood memories might be particularly revealing, he sometimes decided not to tell everything he knew, with the result that we are given only part of the story and have to speculate about what might remain hidden.

Despite these caveats, Freud offered indispensable information about himself, of a kind that fits in well with the general psychoanalytic project of understanding how the mind gets to be the way it is. In part, this is because of a particularly strange and engaging aspect of psychoanalytic history. Psychoanalysis started as a very personal project. Freud literally invented it, and while he drew on lots of already existing ideas (for instance, about the existence of the unconscious), he gave it the stamp of his own remarkable synthesizing ability and personality. This is what is so revolutionary about the first really great psychoanalytic text, Freud's *The Interpretation of Dreams*.[2] Published with the date 1900 imprinted on it (though it was still 1899), this book can be seen as one of the intellectual and cultural building blocks of the twentieth century, the moment at which modern western individuals were invited to think of themselves as having a meaningful "inner life." It was presented as a scientific document, as Freud saw it when he wrote it, and it has all the characteristics of such a work. These include a literature review (now, of course, outdated) and a strong academic framework containing a complex and somewhat tedious neuropsychological model of dreaming. But what is really at the heart of the book is a large set of dreams that Freud subjected to analysis. Nearly fifty of these dreams were his own (most of the others were reported by his patients), providing a great source of information about Freud himself, along with an ironic commentary about the nature of science once psychoanalysis came on the scene.

What is the science of the mind? Something that starts with the dreams of its inventor. And not just any random dreams, but especially embarrassing ones. Here is a famous example, from the end of a dream that Freud reported in a section of the book called "Infantile Material as a Source of Dreams" (the dream itself is in italics):

> *I was in front of the station, but this time in the company of an elderly gentleman. I thought of a plan for remaining unrecognized; and then*

> *saw that this plan had already been put into effect. It was as though thinking and experiencing were one and the same thing. He appeared to be blind, at all events with one eye, and I handed him a male glass urinal (which we had to buy or had bought in town). So I was a sick-nurse and had to give him the urinal because he was blind. If the ticket-collector were to see us like that, he would be certain to let us get away without noticing us. Here the man's attitude and his micturating penis appeared in plastic form.* (This was the point at which I awoke, feeling a need to micturate.)[3]

Freud offered quite an extended analysis of the series of dreams of which this is a part, noting along the way that one source for them is "an absurd megalomania which had long been suppressed in my waking life and a few of whose ramifications had even made their way into the dream's manifest content."[4] This megalomania turned out to be very important, linked to the specific interpretation that Freud gave for the part of the dream quoted here—or rather, to the childhood memory that is associated with it:

> When I was seven or eight years old there was another domestic scene, which I can remember very clearly. One evening before going to sleep I disregarded the rules which modesty lays down and obeyed the calls of nature in my parents' bedroom while they were present. In the course of his reprimand, my father let fall the words: "The boy will come to nothing." This must have been a frightful blow to my ambition, for references to this scene are still constantly recurring in my dreams and are always linked with an enumeration of my achievements and successes, as though I wanted to say: "You see, I *have* come to something." This scene, then, provided the material for the final episode of the dream, in which—in revenge, of course—the roles were interchanged. The older man (clearly my father, since his blindness in one eye referred to his unilateral glaucoma) was now micturating in front of me, just as I had in front of him in my childhood. In the

> reference to his glaucoma I was reminding him of the cocaine, which had helped him in the operation, as though I had in that way kept my promise. Moreover, I was making fun of him; I had to hand him the urinal because he was blind, and I revelled in allusions to my discoveries in connection with the theory of hysteria, of which I felt so proud.[5]

There are a number of aspects of this passage that need unpacking so it can be understood fully, but the key point is how self-justificatory it is. Freud recalled embarrassing himself by urinating in his parents' bedroom and receiving his father's admonishment as a result. An additional piece of background information here is that Freud was seen by both his parents, but especially his mother, as exceptionally gifted. He was her "golden Sigi" (Sigi being the diminutive of Sigismund), her first child, and he had enormous privileges over his many other siblings, as we will discover. His parents predicted—correctly, as it turned out—that he would become a great man. Yet his own recollection was of his father saying, "The boy will come to nothing," and Freud acknowledged that this single denigration had stayed with him, continuing to haunt his dreams and fuel his ambition. Despite his father's prediction, Freud had accomplished a great deal. In fact, he discovered the anesthetic properties of cocaine, which had helped his father through the operation for glaucoma; and even more than that, he had also discovered the meaning of dreams. For Freud also tells us, in the Preface to the second edition of *The Interpretation of Dreams*, that writing this book was a means through which he came to terms with his father's death, as he put it, "the most important event, the most poignant loss, of a man's life."[6] We learn from this that Freud continued to feel a need to prove himself in the face of his father's apparent disparagement. It also shows that he felt ambivalent about his achievements. They were associated with doing much better than his father had ever done, and so were a source of guilt.

In another piece, *An Autobiographical Study* (1925), Freud gives us some of his genealogy:

> I was born on May 6th, 1856, at Freiberg in Moravia, a small town in what is now Czechoslovakia. My parents were Jews, and I have remained a Jew myself. I have reason to believe that my father's family were settled for a long time on the Rhine (at Cologne), that, as a result of a persecution of the Jews during the fourteenth or fifteenth century, they fled eastwards, and that, in the course of the nineteenth century, they migrated back from Lithuania through Galicia into German Austria.[7]

In some ways, this passage is typical of Freud's writing. In it, he acknowledges his Jewish origins and asserts his continued Jewish allegiance. On the other hand, as historian Sander Gilman notes, Freud subtly introduced into this account the suggestion that he was both an Eastern European Jew and *not* an Eastern European Jew.[8] His predecessors might have come from Lithuania and Galicia, but originally they were from the more civilized Rhineland. This can again be seen as an indication of Freud's ambition, but also of an embarrassment that was culturally very common: the rejection of the "low class" *Östjuden* (Eastern European Jews) in order to assert that, Jewish or not, he had a more sophisticated background. That said, Freud's refusal to renege on his Jewish heritage and the openness with which he continued to declare it even amid growing antisemitism, was an example of his combativeness and his lifelong adherence to his principles. The fact that he seemed never to have been tempted to convert to Christianity like several of his contemporaries—the musician Gustav Mahler among them—is one of many indications that Freud would never be told what to do. Regardless of whether embarrassment was one source of his ambition, self-belief and personal integrity were definitely others.

Freud's family was indeed a Jewish one. His father Jacob, a not very successful wool merchant, had originally come from an orthodox Jewish family. By the time Sigmund was born, however, his father had left behind most of his orthodox practices and been exposed to the Jewish "enlightenment." This took material form in a book, the Philippson Bible, which Jacob first bought in 1848, the year of massive revolutions in Europe. Later, he had it rebound and inserted a Hebrew inscription into it for Freud's 35th birthday. This Bible was particularly interesting because of its non-traditional nature. Along with the presentation of the Hebrew text with a parallel German translation, it contained a commentary drawing on modern Bible scholarship and criticism, and not solely on classical Jewish texts. For Freud, this work was a very powerful childhood memory. In his *Autobiographical Study*, he wrote, "My deep engrossment in the Bible story (almost as soon as I had learnt the art of reading) had, as I recognized much later, an enduring effect upon the direction of my interest."[9] Certainly, he identified intensely with Joseph (the Biblical interpreter of dreams) and Moses; and he also dedicated the last major work of his life, *Moses and Monotheism*, to a study of Judaism. But what this particular Bible indicates is something that may or may not have been true of Jacob but was definitely true of Sigmund: a strong affiliation with Jewish culture and identity, without traditional (or in Sigmund's case *any*) religious belief, and with a parallel absorption in western culture as well.

An example here is the series of dreams in *The Interpretation of Dreams* known as the "Rome" dreams. Freud remarked of one of these dreams:

> Another time someone led me to the top of a hill and showed me Rome half-shrouded in mist; it was so far away that I was surprised at my view of it being so clear. There was more in the content of this dream than I feel prepared to detail; but the theme of 'the promised land seen from afar' was obvious in it.[10]

Various issues are relevant to this interpretation, including Freud's mixed feelings about getting further in life than his father ever did. But what is particularly noticeable is that a classical *western* image, that of Rome, is fused with a traditional Jewish and Biblical reference—Moses' failure to enter the Promised Land. It is as if either Freud re-read his Jewish background in European terms (Canaan becomes Rome), or the other way around—that classical European images were imagined in Jewish terms (Rome becomes the Biblical "Promised Land").

Freud was certainly well-educated in both traditions. Not only were the Philippson Bible and Bible stories generally among his first and most loved reading material, but he was also taught Judaism by his rabbi, the inspirational Samuel Hammerschlag, whom Freud remained grateful to and fond of his whole life. His later claim that he barely even recognized Hebrew when he saw it seems unlikely, especially given the trouble that his father took to assemble a "melitza" (a compendium of Biblical quotations) in Hebrew to write into the flyleaf of his gift of the rebound family Bible for Freud's 35th birthday. Even though the Freud family "spoke German and ignored such observances as kashrut and the Sabbath," once they had moved to Vienna when Freud was three years old, they still observed some major Jewish holidays, and some scholars claim that Freud would still have heard his father's "adept … Hebrew recitation of the Passover service."[11] However, he was also extremely well-educated in secular subjects. Psychoanalyst and historian George Makari writes that Freud "proved an extraordinary student" at his school, the Leopoldstädter Gymnasium. "Schooled in Latin and Greek and the classics such as Ovid, Horace, Cicero, Virgil, Sophocles, Homer, and Plato, he quickly made his way to the front of his class."[12] His languages were especially strong: Greek, Latin, Italian, French, English, and Spanish, self-taught as a teenager with his childhood friend Eduard Silberstein. The two boys pretended to be two dogs in a story by the Spanish writer Miquel de Cervantes so that they could communicate secretly and playfully with one another; later in life, Freud was still able to read Spanish well enough to respond to Mexican correspondents.[13] On top of this, Freud was talented in science, the direction he finally took after having played with the idea of becoming a lawyer. In any event, we can say that Freud read the European world from the inside and was well-educated in it, yet he also saw it through Jewish eyes. His Jewishness, on the other hand, was shaped from a more "progressive" direction, which meant that he saw it through western eyes. While he perhaps never fully drew together these different strands of his cultural experience—Jewish and European—he also never relinquished either one of them in favor of the other.

Complex Family Ties

An unavoidable aspect of Freud's Jewish identity was antisemitism, and this is a crucial source of psychoanalysis in important ways. Like many other members of the emancipated Jewish middle class, Freud had the benefit of a first-rate education and received through that the promise of absorption in Austrian, German, and European culture in line with his remarkable intellectual abilities. However, despite official emancipation, antisemitism was rife in Austria and escalated throughout Freud's lifetime. It can reasonably be argued that this placed Freud and Jews like him in a marginal position, in which they both idealized their society and felt deeply its hypocrisy in betraying them. Perhaps this was the necessary context for the invention of a discipline so much on the margins of what was acceptable and yet so potent in diagnosing the infidelities of society to itself.

There was, however, a very famous and very personal issue around antisemitism that seems to have shadowed Freud's relationship with his father. The source for this is once again Freud himself, in the set of associations to the Rome dreams in *The Interpretation of Dreams*, just after the passage mentioned earlier. In this instance, Freud traced his difficulty in getting to Rome to his identification with Hannibal, who "had been the favourite hero of [my] school days." This identification is linked explicitly with antisemitism:

> When in the higher classes I began to understand for the first time what it meant to belong to an alien race, and antisemitic feelings amongst the other boys warned me that I must take up a definite position, the figure of the Semitic general rose still higher in my esteem. To my youthful mind Hannibal and Rome symbolized the conflict between the tenacity of Jewry and the organization of the Catholic church. And the increasing importance of the effects of the antisemitic movement upon our emotional life helped to fix the thoughts and findings of those early days.[14]

Following through these associations, Freud came up with what he described as "the event in my childhood whose power was still being shown in all these emotions and dreams," and which resonated throughout his life. This is the memory of the moment when antisemitism brought his father down to size, and Freud took on the mantle of avenger.

> I may have been ten or twelve years old, when my father began to take me with him on his walks and reveal to me in his talk his views upon things in the world we live in. Thus it was, on one such occasion, that he told me a story to show how much better things were now than they had been in his days. "When I was a young man," he said, "I went for a walk one Saturday in the streets of your birthplace; I was well dressed and had a new fur cap on my head. A Christian came up to me and with a single blow knocked off my cap into the mud and shouted 'Jew! Get off the pavement!'" "And what did you do?" I asked. "I went into the roadway and picked up my cap," was his quiet reply. This struck me as unheroic conduct on the part of the big, strong man who was holding the little boy by the hand. I contrasted this situation with another which fitted my feelings better: the scene in which Hannibal's father, Hamilcar

> Barca, made his boy swear before the household altar to take vengeance on the Romans. Ever since that time Hannibal has had a place in my phantasies.[15]

Psychoanalytically speaking, this memory links Freud's resilience in the face of antisemitism with the idea of avenging or even surpassing his father. Freud's not infrequent ambivalence about Jews was also presumably connected to this sense of his father's weakness. This ambivalence was sometimes expressed forcefully toward his fellow Jewish analysts, and was not limited to his youthful and culturally reinforced antagonism toward the Eastern European Jews from which his mother's family came. In this respect, as critic Daniel Boyarin points out in a book on Jewish masculinity that took Freud's phrase "unheroic conduct" as its title, the gloss Freud put on this memory also represents an attempt to distance himself from the "feminized" aspects of Jewish identity.[16] The vision of the ideal Jewish male as scholarly and weak, rather than as physical and tough, was a conventional version of masculinity in rabbinic Judaism. Here, and in much of his writing, Freud seemed to adopt the view that such "femininity" is to be despised and that true heroism—true manliness—is to be found in strength. Thus, without reducing Freud's relationship with his Jewish identity to something based solely on unresolved Oedipal issues, it is plausible to argue that part of the emotional investment he had in Jewish *achievement*, particularly in the face and context of antisemitic attacks, might be related to his perception of his father as a failed hero, and of Jewish passivity in general as a sign of "racial" disrepute.

In this respect, another "humiliation," as Elisabeth Roudinesco describes it, came in 1865, when Jacob Freud's brother Josef was arrested and imprisoned for possessing counterfeit bank notes. This event recurs in Freud's "Dream of Uncle Josef with the Yellow Beard," which he recounted in *The Interpretation of Dreams*, commenting, "My father, whose hair turned grey from grief in a few days, used always to say that Uncle Josef was not a bad man but only a simpleton."[17] The context for this dream was Freud's anxiety that he would be denied a professorship because of antisemitism, again linking these male Jewish figures with ineffectuality.

Arguably, however, the most important thing about Freud's family background was not its cultural position—though of course, this mattered greatly—but its genealogical complexity. His father Jacob was born in 1815, so was forty-one when Sigmund was born in 1856. By then, Jacob had been married twice, once to Sally Kanner, with whom he had two sons, Emanuel and Philipp, born in 1833 and 1834, respectively, as well as two other children who died in infancy. When Sally died in 1852, he had a brief marriage to a woman called Rebekka, of whom little is known, and then in 1855 he married Amalia Nathanson. Amalia was only twenty at the time, and outlived her husband by thirty-four years. Within a year of the marriage, Amalia had her first child, Schlomo Sigismund (named after Jacob's father who had recently died). That was the "golden Sigi," born on May 6, 1856. He was followed by seven other children in ten years. All but one of these (Julius, who died in infancy in 1858) survived. This meant that Sigmund was born to an "elderly" father and had two half-brothers old enough to be his father and older than his mother. He also had outlived a potentially rivalrous younger brother (whose death he believed to be of crushing importance), was surrounded by sisters (only the youngest surviving sibling—Alexander—was a boy), and in his first ten years of life had a mother who was permanently either pregnant or had just given birth. Additionally, young Sigmund's most intimate friend and playmate was a nephew who was older than him (John, Emanuel's son), and the generational overlaps might also have provoked fantasies in Freud that his mother and older brother were in love, or were better matched than his mother and father.

We probably do not need psychoanalysis to speculate about the lasting effects of this complicated situation. In any event, it is perhaps not surprising, given this tangled web, that Freud would become interested in teasing out family relationships and unspoken wishes and desires. Once again, he himself was a good commentator on these complexities, when thinking about how his early experiences of friendship influenced his later relationships, especially with men:

> I have already shown how my warm friendships as well as my enmities with contemporaries went back to my relations in childhood with a nephew who was a year my senior; how he was my superior, how I early learned to defend myself against him, how we were inseparable friends, and how, according to the testimony of our elders, we sometimes fought with each other and made complaints to them about each other … My emotional life has always insisted that I should have an intimate friend and a hated enemy. I have always been able to provide myself afresh with both, and it has not infrequently happened that the ideal situation of childhood has been so completely reproduced that friend and enemy have come together in a single individual—though not, of course, both at once or with constant oscillations, as may have been the case in my early childhood.[18]

We shall return to Freud's friends and enemies later, but it is instructive to see how he found the source of what he recognized as a repeated pattern in his closeness with this nephew-friend from early life. Friends who turn into enemies were a regular story for Freud, though it is not clear that this ever happened the other way around.

Freud's mother undoubtedly adored and preferred her son over his siblings, but given the nature of her repeated "confinements," she could not have been very available to him in his early life. One consequence of this seemed to be a very strong attachment he had to a nanny or nursemaid, described by Roudinesco as "elderly, ugly, and hardly desirable: just the opposite of Amalia. But she brought the boy affection and sensuality."[19] This nursemaid, variously called Resi Wittek or Monika Zajik, took Freud to church (perhaps to encourage Christian belief in the young Jew) and apparently was his "first instructress" in sensual matters. Freud appeared to have been deeply attached to her, so must have been doubly bereft when, while his mother was having his baby sister Anna in 1858, the nursemaid was accused of theft and put in prison, at Philipp's behest.

By 1860, Jacob's older sons had gone to live in Manchester in England, and the rest of the family had moved to Vienna, to the Jewish area of Leopoldstrasse. Although Jacob was never a successful businessman, the family managed to survive, partly through help from Emanuel and Philipp. Indeed, Roudinesco claims that "After having been the embodiment of strong paternal authority, Jacob now came across as a weak, humiliated man," an assessment supported by Freud's memory of the hat in the gutter episode.[20] The family were not well off and were living in overcrowded conditions; only Sigmund had his own room, perhaps because he was for many years the only boy but more likely because of the preference that his parents showed him over his siblings. Both parents, not just Amalia, were impressed with his capabilities. Jacob famously quipped one day that "My Sigmund's little toe is cleverer than my head. But he would never dare to contradict me," neatly expressing both the authoritarian-patriarchal nature of the traditional Jewish family and its admiring investment in the next generation.[21] This investment would be brought to fruition through the classic route by which Jewish sons surpass their fathers: education and intellectual success. The parental preference meant that nothing would be allowed to interfere with Freud's studies; for example, there is this revealing episode related by biographer Peter Gay:

> When, intent on his school books, he complained about the noise that Anna's piano lessons were making, the piano vanished never to return. It was much regretted by his sister and his mother alike, but without apparent rancor. The Freuds must have been among the very few middle-class Central European families without a

> piano, but that sacrifice faded in the face of the glorious career they imagined for the studious, lively schoolboy in his cabinet.[22]

Among the other points of note about this, there is a link with Freud's lifelong ambivalence about music, which he felt was an art form that psychoanalysis could not really comment upon. But the main issue is simply that whatever Freud wanted in the heated environment of his family, he would get; and his position of dominance over most of his siblings continued throughout his life.

Freud's excellent achievements in school—he stated in *An Autobiographical Study* that, "At the 'Gymnasium' [Grammar School] I was at the top of my class for seven years; I enjoyed special privileges there, and had scarcely ever to be examined in class"—meant that he progressed smoothly toward university studies.[23] Decision-making was left to him, as a reflection of his parents' deference toward his intellectual ability, and he wavered for a while before deciding that medicine would be his choice, if not exactly his "calling":

> Neither at that time, nor indeed in my later life, did I feel any particular predilection for the career of a doctor. I was moved, rather, by a sort of curiosity, which was, however, directed more towards human concerns than towards natural objects; nor had I grasped the importance of observation as one of the best means of gratifying it. My deep engrossment in the Bible story (almost as soon as I had learnt the art of reading) had, as I recognized much later, an enduring effect upon the direction of my interest. Under the powerful influence of a school friendship with a boy rather my senior who grew up to be a well-known politician, I developed a wish to study law like him and to engage in social activities. At the same time, the theories of Darwin, which were then of topical interest, strongly attracted me, for they held out hopes of an extraordinary advance in our understanding of the world; and it was hearing Goethe's beautiful essay on Nature read aloud at a popular lecture by Professor Carl Brühl just before I left school that decided me to become a medical student.[24]

This description of how he ended up as a doctor is very revealing, not just as a plausible account of the thought processes of a romantic, intelligent boy with a tendency to idealize and the ambition to model himself on great thinkers (Darwin, Goethe), but also as a straw in the wind for psychoanalysis itself. Famously, if possibly apocryphally, Freud claimed that, "We do analysis for two reasons: to understand the unconscious and to make a living"—not to treat people and heal them but, as he noted, out of "a sort of curiosity."[25] This shows how Freud, despite his strong grounding in what we would now call the "humanities," saw himself as first and foremost a scientist. Studying medicine was to be a way into the wonders of studying "nature," both animal and human. As we shall see in the next chapter, the journey from here to psychoanalysis was a long one, taking over twenty years. It left its traces, but it was also a mark of Freud's strength of purpose and mind that when the break with existing science came, it was a radical one.

2

Freud before Psychoanalysis

Nineteenth-century psychology was a tumultuous affair, enacting many of the philosophical and scientific disputes of an era in which vast changes occurred in technology, science, and the humanities. In the end, many of the assumptions and expectations of the era were dramatically undermined by the radical shifts in politics and society that took place in the early twentieth century. These were most notably due to the watershed of the First World War, but also the revolutionary consciousness that had spread in one way or another from the French Revolution, through the European insurrections of 1848, to the Bolshevik Revolution of 1917. After this time, it became harder to see the continuities of the post-watershed world with the "Victorians," but these continuities exist and many of the debates and disputes that took place then could be seen resurfacing later.

In the domain of psychology, which is the easiest context in which to place the "pre-psychoanalytic" Freud, the recurrent and still existing fault lines surround such issues as the place of heredity, the degree to which psychologists can rely on personal reports to study subjective experiences, and the impact of researchers on the phenomena they are investigating. This last point is a contentious methodological problem: how can we reliably study psychological events when they are so prone to be influenced by "suggestion," meaning that the expectations, actions, and verbalizations of the researcher are very likely to influence the research subject's responses? *Hypnotic* suggestion is a classic instance of this, and was one of the problems that emerged late in the nineteenth century around some remarkable theatrical demonstrations of hysteria that enormously influenced Freud's thinking. Were hysterical phenomena, in which, seemingly without awareness, patients displayed dramatic physical, as well as mental symptoms, "real," or were they suggested by the doctor who encouraged their performance? The interpenetration of observer and observed, or doctor and patient, also has a more profound significance for the emergence of psychoanalysis in showing how difficult it is to keep to an idea of psychology as fully objective—a "science of behavior," as many would still like it to be—when it arises so potently from personal concerns, and has such strongly personal effects.

Freud's early career marked him out as an able laboratory scientist who under many circumstances would have had a promising research or university career ahead of him. After completing his medical degree at the University of Vienna in 1881, he worked in several zoological and physiological laboratories with some of the best researchers of the time, all of whom reinforced in Freud a materialist orientation that would never leave him. This is very important to hold in mind, because there are times when psychoanalysis can seem ungrounded, speculative, and even "mystical" in its formulations, with "occult" interests and influences upon it. Nevertheless, at root it is a materialist doctrine. Freud was convinced that there are real psychological forces at work within the mind, even if they cannot always be directly known (this is what makes some of them "unconscious"), giving it a lawful structure and a degree of predictability, and requiring careful observation and investigation of a kind not dissimilar to any other scientific approach.

In addition to his scientific studies at university, Freud had also taken a philosophy course with an important figure, German philosopher and psychologist Franz Brentano. While antagonistic to introspection as an approach to "privileged" knowledge of our thoughts and feelings (i.e., he believed we are no more accurate in our account of ourselves and our thoughts, motivations, and inner life than we are in our account of others), Brentano was committed to the idea that "inner perception" was important. As George Makari explains:

> Inner perception might not be objective, but it remained a critical starting point for any psychology. Luckily, human memory allowed for the recollection and examination of these transitory moments. In addition to emphasizing the stabilizing power of memory, Brentano called for a close study of language and gesture as a way of aiding our knowledge of another's inner world. Psychologists should also pay special attention to children and animals, as well as diseased mental states and weird psychological occurrences, he advised.[1]

Freud followed many of these recommendations (though not the one about observing animals), somewhat leavening his materialism without reducing his commitment to the scientific process, which, like Brentano, he saw as a direct and progressive development of philosophy.

The laboratories in which Freud worked included that of chemist and naturalist Carl Claus, where Freud famously examined the gonads of eels, hunting for any evidence of testicles (he found none); and then with Ernst Wilhelm von Brücke, another visionary scientist whose work in developing laboratory-based science was of lasting importance. Makari's summary of this period is instructive:

> For the next six years [from 1876], Freud toiled in Brücke's lab, happily examining nerve cells. He made some minor discoveries, developed a new stain, and by the age of twenty-six could boast of a number of publications from his work. In the middle of these studies, Freud served a year of compulsory military service, during which time, to keep himself occupied, he translated some essays by John Stuart Mill on subjects like the emancipation of woman. Returning to Vienna, he finally sat for his medical exams in 1881,

> seven and a half years after he began his medical education and two and a half years longer than the average student. Freud passed and later attributed his success to his extraordinary memory, since he had not bothered to thoroughly prepare himself.[2]

By 1882, Freud had shown himself competent in laboratory science and committed to hard work and the systematic advancement of neurology. He also had a sideline interest both in philosophy and in translation. Although medically qualified, he was not committed to a medical career; he was clearly ambitious but also much more interested in knowledge than in treatment, or even (at least at this stage) in financial gains. Indeed, *lack* of money characterized this period in his life and recurred later, especially in the difficult period after the First World War. This is perhaps worth remembering, both as an antidote to the conventional vision of psychoanalysis as an affluent profession, and as a source of the political sensitivity Freud always had toward the poor and to the progressive principles of social democracy. At this stage, however, it might not have mattered too much, except that Freud unexpectedly fell in love. The immediate consequence was that he realized (and Brücke confirmed this, if for no other reason than that his two very able assistants were senior to Freud) that if he was to earn enough money to be able to get married, he would have to leave the research lab and take up his fall-back profession of medicine. It was this need for financial stability that pushed Freud to become as much a therapist as an investigator. This combined role was essential to the emergence of psychoanalysis as a subject based on practice rather than theoretical knowledge, but even more strongly, a discipline in which the doctor–patient encounter would become the principal way in which knowledge would be produced. Being forced out of the laboratory and into work with patients, first in the hospital in Vienna and then in private practice, was crucial for Freud's development into the world's first psychoanalyst.

But let us return briefly to Freud's love affair. After all, psychoanalysis is largely a practice of love—the love of the patient for the analyst, revealing the hidden passion of the patient and the unconscious conflicts that follow from this. Psychoanalysis is one of those practices that dares to speak love's name clearly and openly, along with an appreciation of its embodiment in sex, the material grounding of the lofty romantic visions to which people are prone, and through which they deceive themselves. In Freud's case, this love was indeed lofty and romantic, and also quite mundane. His sister Anna was engaged to Eli Bernays, who came from a prestigious, though not wealthy, Jewish family in Vienna, with a good orthodox pedigree including some major ancestral rabbis. The families mixed and on a visit in 1882, at the age of twenty-six, Freud met Eli's sister Martha, and was smitten by her. Elisabeth Roudinesco makes an arresting point about this:

> Since the time ten years earlier when he had had strong feelings for Gisela Fluss [a young girl he knew at the time—Freud was actually more taken with her mother], he had taken very little interest in young women. Suffering from inhibitions, anxiety, and neurasthenia, he periodically succumbed to somatic ailments: dizziness, fainting spells, cardiac and digestive disorders, migraines, inflammatory neuralgias, colitis .... Under the onslaught of physical pain, this tireless worker quickly became a regular user of nicotine, first smoking cigarettes and then cigars, some twenty a day.[3]

All of this is to say that Freud did not learn about sex and sexuality from wide personal experience. He tended to bottle up these feelings, and we might say—thinking psychoanalytically, as we are perhaps allowed to do in Freud's case—that he became neurotic as a result. Indeed, his hypochondriasis and psychosomatism were quite pronounced throughout his life and may always have had something to do with sexual inhibition, despite the openness of his writings about sex. Smoking, too, was a long-term theme and if it substituted for sexuality, it rapidly became one of the central sustaining forces of Freud's life—and, of course, one of the most destructive too, eventuating in the cancer of the jaw from which he would suffer deeply for over twenty years.

In any event, Freud's love for Martha was conventional and romantic, and it developed very fast. He met her in April 1882; sent her a rose and a Latin verse the next day; and by June 17, the couple had agreed secretly (i.e., without the knowledge of their parents) to marry. A famously long engagement then followed, spread over four years while Freud was irritably seeking enough professional success to be able to make a reliable and sufficiently substantial income. He visited Martha where she was living in Wandsbek, near Hamburg, several times during this period; but these visits were not that frequent, and Freud and Martha had to resort to writing letters to sustain and develop their relationship. In this medium, Freud was and remained a star: his letters to Martha are hectoring at times, conventional and romantic to a fault, open and bossy, but also and always full of life. This is what he wrote just two days after the engagement, on June 19, 1882:

> My precious, most beloved girl
> I knew it was only after you had gone that I would realize the full extent of my happiness and, alas! the degree of my loss as well. I still cannot grasp it, and if that elegant little box and that sweet picture were not lying in front of me, I would think it was all a beguiling dream and be afraid to wake up. Yet friends tell me it's true, and I myself can remember details more charming, more mysteriously enchanting than any dream phantasy could create. It must be true. Martha is mine, the sweet girl of whom everyone speaks with admiration, who despite all my resistance captivated my heart at our first meeting, the girl I feared to court and who came toward me with high-minded confidence, who strengthened the faith in

> my own value and gave me new hope and energy to work when I needed it most.
>
> When you return, darling girl, I shall have conquered the shyness and awkwardness which have hitherto inhibited me in your presence. We will sit alone in that nice little room again, my girl will settle down in the brown armchair (out of which we were so suddenly startled yesterday), I at her feet on the round stool, and we will talk of the time when there will be no difference between night and day, when neither intrusions from without nor farewells nor worries shall keep us apart.[4]

Given the later reputation of this marriage as dull and bourgeois, with Martha in charge of the domestic domain but outside the sphere of everything exciting and creative in Freud's life, it is worth taking note of the uncertainty in this letter and in many others, and the idealization of Martha as an admired and confident "sweet girl" (she was twenty-one). Freud's later correspondence with others was also sometimes emphatic and intense—his male colleagues Wilhelm Fliess and Carl Jung are the best examples—but this does not mean that his feelings for Martha were anything but genuine.

Difficult as it clearly was to manage the separation and the sexual abstinence that went with it (some evidence of this might be read backwards from the fact that once they were married, Freud and Martha had six children in nine years), the long engagement did allow Freud to continue his training and preparation to be the great inventor or discoverer that he became, traveling through parts of Europe and attaching himself to various new possibilities in the interests of making a name for himself. And perhaps the sexual restrictions were not quite so problematic for Freud as we might assume. As Roudinesco notes, he had always been awkward and uncertain with women. Later, observing the strain that repeated childbearing had on Martha, and unhappy with the contraceptive methods of the time, Freud tried sexual abstinence—first in 1893, and then more lastingly after the birth of their youngest child, Anna, in 1895. We know this from his letters to Fliess. Roudinesco comments, rather tartly, "The sex life of the greatest modern theoretician of sexuality thus presumably lasted nine years." She found no evidence for various theories of Freud's hidden wild sexuality that have entertained some writers: "In reality, on several occasions Freud attempted to renew his carnal relations with Martha. But he felt old and awkward, and he finally gave up."[5]

An exception here, however, might be Martha's sister Minna, who Freud was very attached to, as can be seen from numerous quite passionate letters that he wrote to her (among other things, she was his ally in his courtship of Martha, whereas Martha's mother rather disapproved of him). Four years younger than Martha, she was already engaged in 1882 to Ignaz Schönberg, a young Viennese to whom Freud became close. Schönberg was a very promising student of philosophy, but by mid-1885 he had contracted tuberculosis and had broken off his engagement to Minna to "free" her; he died in February 1886. Minna was only twenty-one, but she never married and instead was drawn into the Freud family circle, eventually coming to live with Freud and Martha and their six young children in 1896. From then on, she shared domestic duties with Martha, but she was also a friend and confidante to Freud. She corrected the proofs of his work, and her wit and liveliness seem to have been greater than that of her elder sister. Freud took holidays with her, including one now-famous trip in 1898 when he apparently signed them into a guesthouse in Switzerland as "*Dr. Sigm. Freud u Frau* (Dr. Sigm. Freud & wife)." This entry, plus a claim made in 1957 by Jung (Freud's erstwhile close follower and then enemy, whose testimony is unlikely to be reliable), and other sources, have led some critics to believe that Freud had an affair with Minna in the 1890s, at the time when he had withdrawn sexually from his wife. There is little evidence in any correspondence of such an affair, and Roudinesco, following in the main tradition of Freud's biographers, is scathing about it; but others are fairly convinced, and while conclusive "proof" of the affair is not available, it has not been reliably refuted. Whether it is important is another matter. "Did Freud have a sexual secret?" seems to be a common concern of many writers on the topic, as if it would not be possible for the inventor of psychoanalysis to be as "celibate" as he appeared to be. What no one sensible has suggested is that he had a "wild" sexual life, whether or not he had a sexual relationship with his sister-in-law. What is also evident is that even as Freud revealed a great deal about himself in his writings and to his friends, he also held back quite a lot, usually consciously, echoing a psychoanalytic observation that each of us has, needs, and in most respects is entitled to, a private life.

In Search of Professional Development

Before returning to Freud's professional trajectory, it is worth noting one peculiarity of his emotional investment in Martha. It is widely claimed, and seems to be true, that Freud prohibited Martha any overt Jewish religious practices, including lighting Shabbat candles and having their sons circumcised, even though, because of legal necessity, they had a (Reform) Jewish wedding. Yet in a long and fascinating letter he wrote to Martha early in their engagement (on July 23, 1882), Freud was clearly basking in the "yichus"—that is, the prestige—of her rabbinical ancestors. He describes going to see a stationer in Hamburg, an orthodox Jew who took a liking to Freud and who—without knowing of Freud's connection—spoke with great praise and respect of "a certain Bernays" who had become the rabbi of the area. Freud details some of the reasons why Rabbi Bernays was exceptional, including his willingness to expound rationally on Jewish law rather than treat it as dogma and his acceptance of enjoyment as a valuable aspect of life. He concluded this letter with the following short paean both to Martha and to her grandfather.

> When I took my leave I was more deeply moved than the Old Jew could possibly guess … If my Marty wishes to take with her to Vienna some gifts in the form of notepaper, she must go to the Adolphsplatz, to our old Jew, disciple of her grandfather, and mention her name. Let him see that the stock of his master has not deteriorated since he sat at his feet. And as for us, this is what I believe: even if the form wherein the old Jews were happy no longer offers us any shelter, something of the core, of the essence of this meaningful and life-affirming Judaism will not be absent from our home.[6]

The idea with which this letter closes is one that Freud stayed true to throughout his life: that even though he had no religious belief and could not identify formally with most aspects of Judaism and Jewish culture (later, including Zionism), his attachment to his Jewish identity remained. There was something in it that offered a stable and meaningful core to his emotional life.

During the period of Freud and Martha's engagement, there were two particularly formative experiences for Freud that had a lasting effect on his professional life. The first was the drug cocaine, which Freud first read about as a treatment for morphine dependence and then tried on himself, becoming convinced of its extraordinary anesthetic and therapeutic properties. "Discovering" cocaine in this way seemed to Freud at the time to be exactly what he needed. It would make him known, set him toward professional advancement, and make it possible to marry his fiancée. Soon after his first experiments with the drug, Freud published an article about it and widely recommended its use, especially as an anesthetic. He also used cocaine personally for a long time—probably right through the 1890s—to stimulate wakefulness and feed his habit of frenzied work until very late at night. However, whereas Freud believed that cocaine had no addictive qualities or side effects of its own, the truth very rapidly was revealed to be otherwise, and in a personally devastating way. His older colleague in Brücke's laboratory, the very distinguished scientist Ernst Fleischl von Marxow, was addicted to morphine as a result of taking the drug to deal with the pain caused by an amputated thumb. Freud encouraged him to take cocaine to help wean himself off morphine, but the result was an addiction to both drugs, which included psychotic experiences due to the psychoactive impact of cocaine. Fleischl von Marxow eventually died in 1891, probably because of this drug addiction; at the very least, Freud's prescription of cocaine had not made things better, and very likely made them worse.

It is possible that the looming awareness of being shown to be foolhardy in relation to cocaine was one reason why Freud applied for a grant in 1885 to allow him to travel to Paris. As Makari states bluntly, "It was a good time for him to get out of town."[7] Irrespective of this, however, a stay in Paris was a good move for a young doctor interested in hysteria and other nervous disorders, because Paris housed, at the Salpêtrière, the greatest and most famous expert on that area of work in those times and indeed most others: Jean-Martin Charcot. Charcot's key concern was to show how, in those predisposed to it by heredity, unconscious ideas of the type revealed by hypnotic suggestion could have physical as well as mental effects, and could be understood as the cause of hysterical symptoms. Freud was completely overwhelmed by Charcot's presence and his ideas. Writing to Martha a couple of months after his arrival in Paris, in November 1885, he presented a picture of himself as utterly transformed by what he had seen during live demonstrations of hypnotic effects on patients and by the extraordinary impact of Charcot himself, who embodied the creative genius that Freud sought to become. He told Martha that he believed himself to be changing, and that this was all thanks to Charcot:

> Charcot, who is one of the greatest of physicians and a man whose common sense borders on genius, is simply wrecking all my aims

> and opinions. I sometimes come out of his lectures as from out of Nôtre Dame, with an entirely new idea about perfection. But he exhausts me; when I come away from him I no longer have any desire to work at my own silly things; it is three whole days since I have done any work, and I have no feelings of guilt. My brain is sated as after an evening in the theatre. Whether the seed will ever bear any fruit, I don't know; but what I do know is that no other human being has ever affected me in the same way.[8]

"No other human being ... " Recall that Freud wrote this to his fiancée! But he was serious, and he took steps to ensure that he would be known to Charcot and could become associated with him. Despite his weak French, he undertook to translate Charcot's lectures on hysteria and hypnosis into German, corresponding with him for some time and becoming a kind of "official," if still junior, representative of his ideas in Vienna. This did not stand Freud wholly in good stead, because Charcot's ideas were not particularly popular in the German-speaking world and became less so as they were attacked by Hippolyte Bernheim. This important French neurologist in Nancy developed an account of suggestion that showed how widespread and normal a phenomenon it was, undermining Charcot's idea that hysterics were hereditarily predisposed. If everyone were susceptible to suggestion, then the hysterical phenomena supposedly revealed by Charcot could very easily have been created by his theatrics—an accusation for which there was some evidence. Without giving up on his support for much of Charcot's teaching, Freud also translated Bernheim, drawing from this work a synthesis in which the power of *unconscious* suggestion was made primary, including (but no longer depending) on hypnosis. Alongside a variety of other perceptions, this had particular value for Freud: it meant that he could focus on "intrapsychic" events (i.e., on psychology) and that he could use the observations that might derive from psychopathology to make sense of the general human condition. From this broad field, much that was central to psychoanalysis would later arise.

Discovering "Creative Strengths and Limitations"

Once married and settled with Martha, with his rapidly growing family around him and with the beginnings of his medical practice, Freud's work increasingly focused on neurosis, especially hysteria, and on the creation of a new way of understanding and treating the large numbers of Viennese women who suffered from this disorder. In this, he was enormously aided by the moral but also very practical and financial support of a highly respected and successful Viennese doctor, Josef Breuer. Fourteen years older than Freud, Breuer had had an outstanding career in neurophysiology and was now the doctor of choice for others in his profession and for many of Vienna's leading families. Freud visited him frequently after his return from Paris, and benefitted greatly from his hospitality and generosity, so much so that he named his first daughter Mathilde, after Breuer's wife. But his main gain was a link with a specific case of hysteria that Breuer had treated in the early 1880s—that of Bertha Pappenheim, who became known to all psychoanalysts as "Anna O," the first patient of the therapy resembling psychoanalysis. Anna/Bertha was twenty-one years old in 1880 when she started to become ill; and by 1881, with the death of her beloved father, who she had been nursing, her symptoms had become extraordinary in their gothic variety and intensity. Breuer's description is worth reading. She had physical seizures, paralysis and rigidities, hallucinations, "absences" of consciousness, and an experience "of having two selves, a real one and an evil one which forced her to behave badly, and so on."[9] She lost her ability to speak and then, most remarkably, developed a kind of selective problem of translation, in which she no longer knew German but did know several other languages. For psychoanalysis, which always has a lot to do with translation of the speech of the unconscious, this was an especially poignant symptom. Just before Anna/Bertha's father died.

> She spoke only in English—apparently, however, without knowing that she was doing so. She had disputes with her nurse who was, of course, unable to understand her. It was only some months later that I [Breuer] was able to convince her that she was talking English. Nevertheless, she herself could still understand the people about her who talked German. Only in moments of extreme anxiety did her power of speech desert her entirely, or else she would use a mixture of all sorts of languages.

After her father died, things got even worse, and as well as being suicidal.

> She now spoke only English and could not understand what was said to her in German. Those about her were obliged to talk to her in English; even the nurse learned to make herself to some extent understood in this way. She was, however, able to read French and Italian. If she had to read one of these aloud, what she produced, with extraordinary fluency, was an admirable extempore English translation.[10]

This pattern of intense hysterical symptoms was very striking, but what made this case especially productive was the therapeutic work that Breuer engaged in with his patient. Serendipitously, he discovered that Anna/Bertha entered a kind of "auto-hypnotic" state each day, in which it was possible to encourage her to put her fantasies and daydreams into words with the effect of making her feel calmer, at least temporarily. After her father died, however, Breuer noted that her thoughts became more compulsive and that the work required to deal with them was harder. He also described some bizarre temporal features. Anna/Bertha presented herself as living through the events of 1882 as if they were 1881—day by day—and sometimes in relation to 1880. But something else Breuer noted was of great significance: that as the original events of 1880 (the period of nursing her father) were brought to light, the symptoms attached to them would disappear.

For example, for a while, Anna/Bertha could not drink, but when she remembered an occasion when she had felt revolted by seeing a dog drinking from a glass, she was cured of this symptom. Breuer's description of the procedure, including his crediting Anna/Bertha with the terminology that later became attached to psychoanalytic treatment, went down in history. He had been seeing her daily, but she had been moved to the countryside so he could not continue to do so for a while.

> While she was in the country, when I was unable to pay her daily visits, the situation developed as follows. I used to visit her in the evening, when I knew I should find her in her hypnosis, and I then relieved her of the whole stock of imaginative products which she had accumulated since my last visit. It was essential that this should be effected completely if good results were to follow. When this was done she became perfectly calm, and next day she would be agreeable, easy to manage, industrious and even cheerful; but on the second day she would be increasingly moody, contrary and unpleasant, and this would become still more marked on the third day. When she was like this it was not always easy to get her to talk, even in her hypnosis. She aptly described this procedure, speaking seriously, as a "talking cure," while she referred to it jokingly as "chimney-sweeping." She knew that after she had given utterance to her hallucinations she would lose all her obstinacy and what she described as her "energy"; and when, after some comparatively long interval, she was in a bad temper, she would refuse to talk, and I was obliged to overcome her unwillingness by urging and pleading and using devices such as repeating a formula with which she was in the habit of introducing her stories. But she would never begin to talk until she had satisfied herself of my identity by carefully feeling my hands.[11]

There is a lot that can be said about this case and no room to deal with it in more detail here. But what can be seen in this quotation is very characteristic of psychoanalysis in the form that Freud later developed it. First, the relationship between doctor and patient is of central importance: Anna/Bertha would only deal with Breuer and no other doctor. This was a highly charged emotional situation. Indeed, Freud later accused Breuer of being afraid of his patient's sexual fantasies about him and of running away from them, and attributed to this Breuer's refusal to accept Freud's theory that sexuality was at the source of all hysterical phenomena (i.e., Breuer was denying the knowledge that he actually had).[12] Second, the treatment depends on *collaboration* between doctor and patient. The memory work does not come simply from suggestion or hypnosis induced by the doctor, but from the patient's capacity to link her current experience with a memory that lies behind it. This gave rise to another famous phrase of Breuer and Freud's, that "hysterics suffer mainly from reminiscences."[13] And third, the activity involved is one of speech—the "talking cure" as it came to be known. It is also not irrelevant that the outcome of Breuer's treatment of Anna/Bertha was an uncertain one. She was clearly not cured of her difficulties and required years of further treatment. Yet she also went on to live an inventive, creative, and influential life as one of the founders of social work and of contemporary feminism; and given the state she was in as a young woman, this must be counted as a success.

The impact of this case on Freud was huge. It prompted him to take up and develop Breuer's "cathartic" approach to therapy, in which talking through the memories underpinning a current symptom would be the central task. He continued to experiment with different forms of hypnosis and suggestion for a while, but by the time the two men published their ground-breaking work *Studies on Hysteria* in 1895, he had already outstripped his mentor's thinking. The book, from which the material on Anna O extracted above is taken, contained this famous case plus four others, all of which were Freud's; and by the end of it, Freud, rather than Breuer, was the one pushing the project along. At the end of the book, Freud also articulated the therapeutic aims of psychoanalysis in a way that has never been bettered. Arguing against therapeutic heroism and with the acid irony that characterized his best writing, Freud shows a realistic appreciation that under conditions of intractable suffering it is still worth doing what we can. He commented as follows to a putative objector:

> "Why, you tell me yourself that my illness is probably connected with my circumstances and the events of my life. You cannot alter these in any way. How do you propose to help me, then?" And I have been able to make this reply: "No doubt fate would find it easier than I do to relieve you of your illness. But you will be able to convince yourself that much will be gained if we succeed in transforming your hysterical misery into common unhappiness. With a mental life that has been restored to health you will be better armed against that unhappiness."[14]

From hysterical misery to common unhappiness: this capacity to learn to "live with one's ailments," yet also clear-sightedly understand what they are about, is part of the moral vision of psychoanalysis, distinguishing it from therapeutic quackery and over-estimation of what any of us can do for one another. Unhappiness is always present, Freud posited, but we can deal with it better if we become capable of speaking and thinking about it properly.

Freud did not behave particularly well toward Breuer, seemingly resenting what he regarded as the older man's lack of wholehearted support for him. In fact, Breuer offered Freud an enormous amount and was extremely important in launching his psychoanalytic career; and he also remained fond of him. Peter Gay summarizes:

> As Freud saw it, he was the explorer who had had the courage of Breuer's discoveries; in pushing them as far as they would go, with all their erotic undertones, he had inevitably alienated the

> munificent mentor who had presided over his early career ... No doubt quite as irritating, Freud owed Breuer money that Breuer did not want him to repay. His disagreeable grumbling about Breuer in the 1890s is a classic case of ingratitude, the resentment of a proud debtor against his older benefactor.[15]

As the break with Breuer was occurring, Freud was becoming increasingly involved with the man who was to become known as the "midwife" of psychoanalysis, Wilhelm Fliess. The two met in 1887, and Freud's "attraction" to him was instant and passionate—indeed, many commentators have seen Fliess as an object of Freud's homosexual, or at least homosocial, desire, something that Freud himself was also alert to.

Fliess was a quirky, intense, and very bright doctor in Berlin, whose ideas now seem almost completely bizarre: theories of nasal-sexual linkage, bisexuality, and biological rhythmicity (including a male twenty-three-day cycle to match the female menstrual one). Throughout the 1890s, the two doctors were in intense correspondence and had several meetings in which their developing theories and ideas were exchanged. Their correspondence was laced with personal and professional concerns intertwined with one another, once again making the point that these are indistinguishable for psychoanalysis. Without understanding Freud's hopes and despairs, his difficulties and his breakthroughs, his fantasies and his inhibitions, we cannot fully understand psychoanalysis at all. Fliess also operated on Freud twice, ostensibly to cure his neurosis, but to no great effect; it seems like he was hoping that by dealing with Freud's nose, he would help him wean himself from cocaine. Indeed, it is fair enough to say, as many have, that Fliess functioned as Freud's "psychoanalyst," and just like many other psychoanalytic relationships, this one ended with the "patient" firmly rejecting the one who had helped him, leaving him, in this case flailing, behind.

Among the many events of the Freud–Fliess years, two stand out for our purposes. One was the *Project for a Scientific Psychology*, which was Freud's "feverish" attempt in 1895 to put psychoanalysis on a firm neurological footing, somewhat in the tradition of the important little book *On Aphasia* that he had written a few years earlier. This attempt was a vast one, growing over several weeks until it could hold no more and collapsed upon itself. Makari concludes:

> In the end, Freud reported that "everything seemed to fall into place, the cogs meshed, I had the impression that the thing now was really a machine that shortly would function on its own." But Frankenstein's monster would never blink its eyes and rise from the lab table. By late November, Freud confessed: "I no longer understand the state of mind in which I hatched the psychology." It was a "kind of madness." He put the draft away and never published it. The "Project" was a trial run that let Freud take the measure of various philosophical and scientific conceptions of the mind. Central to this effort was Freud's experimenting with a Meynert-like linkage of psychology and anatomy, based on his Phi, Psi, and Omega neurons. While such biological grounding seemed to offer tremendous advantages, Freud would ultimately conclude that it glittered like fool's gold.[16]

Some writers have claimed that all Freud's later theories are prefigured in the *Project*, and they may be correct in the sense that he never reneged on his materialist assumptions or on the hope that he would develop a system robust enough to draw together biological, neurological, and psychological thinking. In addition, some basic ideas developed in the *Project*—such as the conservation of energy and the reduction of tension as fundamental principles of mental life—stayed in Freud's thinking for the next four decades. He also remained a synthesizer and systematizer in his work. Indeed, it can be reasonably argued that what marked out his theory of the unconscious from others along similar lines that had gone before or came after, was precisely how he was able to integrate within it such a vast amount of observation and speculation, without the theory ever (quite) collapsing again. So, as Gay writes, "if it is a failure, it is a magnificent one. The *Psychology* does not precisely read like an early draft of psychoanalytic theory, but Freud's ideas on the drives, on repression and defence, on mental economy with its contending forces of energies, and on the human animal as the wishing animal, are all adumbrated here."[17]

The second event has more to do with Fliess and does not show Freud in a good light, yet it was also important for what was to come. Among Freud's patients in 1895 was Emma Eckstein, who suffered from hysterical symptoms and nosebleeds. Freud asked Fliess to operate on her, but after he had returned to Berlin, Emma deteriorated badly and another doctor had to be called in. He very dramatically discovered that Fliess had left a half meter (nearly twenty inches) of gauze in the nose, an act of medical negligence that almost killed her. Freud must have realized just how badly this reflected on his friend, yet he seemed to go out of his way to protect him, even finding a means later to suggest that the bleeding from Emma's nose had actually been due to her own neurosis. "So far I know only that she bled out of *longing*," he wrote in a letter to Fliess, "She has always been a bleeder."[18] Although there was still plenty of intense contact between the two men after this event, from this moment on Freud gradually drifted apart from Fliess. Indeed, some writers make a good case that the famous "Dream of Irma's Injection" from 1895, described more fully in the next chapter, was in large part an attempt by Freud's "unconscious" part to clear Fliess of the blame attached to him for what happened to Emma; and that this might be one reason that Freud did not tell Fliess much about the dream at the time or complete the analysis of that dream in print. In any event, by 1900 it was all over: the two men met for the last time, argued bitterly, and never saw each other again.

Fliess had served his purpose. Freud had needed his interlocutor then as he would need others later, and as patients need their psychoanalysts; and he had discovered a great deal about himself, his relationships with men, and his creative strengths and limitations. It was time for him to get on with what he most needed to do: build his intellectual enterprise and change the world.

3

Dreaming of Psychoanalysis

Psychoanalysis started in the 1890s, and its birth can be traced to the publication of *Studies on Hysteria* in 1895.[1] However, its most dramatic entry into the world came in the twentieth century. The key moment was the publication of *The Interpretation of Dreams*, which actually appeared in 1899 but had 1900 on the flyleaf. This was probably just a marketing tactic by the publisher Franz Deuticke; if so, it was not a particularly successful one as the book sold only a few hundred copies in its first six years. Nevertheless, the choice of date was apposite. The book may have been a slow starter, but it marked the beginning of a movement that in many ways defined the "zeitgeist" (the mood) of the twentieth century, with Freud himself as its emblem and figurehead. After *The Interpretation of Dreams*, the modern world changed. As it became harder to deny the possibility of the existence of the "unconscious," people grew more suspicious of each other's motives and aware of just how little they knew about themselves.

As noted earlier, Freud, writing in the 1908 preface to the second edition of *The Interpretation of Dreams*, commented that it was a product of a very significant personal event. "For this book has a further subjective significance for me personally—a significance which I only grasped after I had completed it. It was, I found, a portion of my own self-analysis, my reaction to my father's death—that is to say, to the most important event, the most poignant loss, of a man's life."[2] As some commentators have pointed out, this was quite an odd thing for Freud to say. His father was certainly an important figure for Freud, but they had not had a lot to do with one another in the

1890s, and while the death of a father is very likely a significant event for any man, it is not necessarily "the most important" one—the death of a mother or some other event could also lay claim to this status. Yet the comment is symptomatic and revealing. Asking the question of why Freud felt his father's death so intensely, philosopher and psychoanalyst Joel Whitebook notes:

> Freud himself came up with a convincing explanation but could not run with it. "In [my] inner self," he told Fliess, "the whole past has been reawakened by this event." In the aftermath of Jacob's death, Freud was plunged into a state of acute mourning and began a systematic self-analysis—which he had previously pursued in a more-or-less ad hoc fashion—in an attempt to come to grips with the pain. This tells us that he had reconciled himself to the fact that what he was suffering from was a form of *psycho*-pathology ... He wrote to Fliess that he had become his own "most important patient" and that his "self-analysis" had become the "essential thing" in his life. Freud's creative illness had reached its peak; sickness, therapy and the pursuit of knowledge now converged in his self-analysis.[3]

In Whitebook's view, Freud's narrow focus on his relationship with his father infiltrated too strongly both the self-analysis and *The Interpretation of Dreams*, pushing his mother and the more intimate, relationship-oriented possibilities of psychoanalysis to one side.

Whether or not this is the case, there is something very striking about the book. Arising as it does from his self-analysis, it is grounded very deeply in Freud's own personality. This breaks down the usual opposition that can be found between "objective" science and "subjective" experience. For Freud, partly following in the philosophical tradition of introspection that had predated the emergence of experimental psychology at the end of the nineteenth century, the invention of his new science was intimately entangled with the capacity for self-reflection and self-knowledge. The status of this self-reflection was sufficiently high for it to form the foundation for scientific understanding. Or to put it more starkly: *The Interpretation of Dreams* stakes a claim to scientific status, and has the accouterments of a scientific report in it (literature review, conceptual chapters, data, etc.). Yet most of its material is deeply subjective—reports of dreams and their interpretation by one man, Freud. Furthermore, many of these dreams—forty-six in all, including most of the important ones—were dreamt by Freud himself. So here we have a book of science, founding a discipline with claims to be scientific, but based on the dream life of just one man. This could be, and indeed has been, a paradox that has prompted many critics to discard psychoanalysis as a figment of Freud's imagination. A more sympathetic point of view could, however, suggest that it raises the issue of what it means to do science in the realm of the "inner life" of a person. Maybe one of Freud's most profound contributions to the twentieth century that he marked so strongly was to suggest that science need not discard human experiences. Rather, to produce a truly scientific psychology in the sense of one that is comprehensive and adequate to the truth, we need also to listen carefully to our dreams.

It is worth noting in passing that *The Interpretation of Dreams* had another quite specific genealogy, relating to the social circumstances under which Freud labored—the emergence of ever-stronger antisemitism in Vienna and his relative isolation from the medical establishment. This led him to present his developing thoughts on dreams not to psychiatric meetings or congresses, but to the Jewish lodge of Vienna, the "B'nai Brith." He was linked with this organization from the mid-1890s onwards, and especially in the period in which the book was germinating. Freud gave a startlingly demanding series of lectures to his lodge, in particular during 1896 and 1897, that became the basis for *The Interpretation of Dreams*. Here is a description (reproduced by Hugo Knoepfmacher) of the reception given to Freud's first lecture to the members, "On Dream Interpretation," on December 7, 1897:

> The minutes of that meeting read: "The high-spirited lecture, involving general human interest, and the masterful presentation which, in spite of the difficulty of the subject, was well adapted to lay understanding, made for a most rewarding evening. The audience showed its gratitude by frantic applause."[4]

Freud was also actively involved in the general work of the lodge. Jerry Diller states that he "attended meetings regularly, was active in recruiting new members and establishing a second Vienna chapter, led discussions on the mission of the order, and delivered twenty-one lectures to the group between 1897 and 1917, mostly before 1902. Except for Fliess and two talks given to the Judische Akademische Lesehalle in 1896 and 1897, the B'nai Brith was his exclusive audience during this period."[5] Indeed, as author Dennis Klein commented, "The Jewish society became an active intellectual forum for his metapsychological views during the productive five-year period 1897–1902, and, in this respect, was a precursor of the movement of psychoanalysis."[6] Freud continued his relationship with the B'nai Brith until the end of the First World War, lecturing to them in April 1915 on "We and Death" and, for the last time in 1917 on "Imagination and Art."

The lack of an alternative platform was a major reason for Freud's engagement with the B'nai Brith, and this engagement withered away once he formed the Wednesday meeting group that eventually became the Psychoanalytic Society. However, Freud was also attracted to the lodge for positive reasons. In a very famous letter to the B'nai Brith written in 1926 in response to its greetings for his seventieth birthday, Freud described why he had found this Jewish group so congenial:

> It happened that in the years after 1895 two strong impressions coincided to produce the same effect on me. On the one hand, I

> had gained the first insight into the depths of human instinct, had seen many things which were sobering, at first even frightening; on the other hand, the disclosure of my unpopular discoveries led to my losing most of my personal relationships at that time; I felt as though outlawed, shunned by all. This isolation aroused in me the longing for a circle of excellent men with high ideals who would accept me in friendship despite my temerity. Your Lodge was described to me as the place where I could find such men.[7]

The reference to "men" is worth noting, as it would be some time before women became involved in psychoanalysis. Once that happened, however, they were very important, marking psychoanalysis as a space for feminism despite the apparent misogyny of some of its theories, and Freud's personal (though also contradictory) conservatism on issues of gender. More to the point, Freud developed a narrative of discovery in which he was (as he noted in the above text) isolated and "outlawed," and only his compatriots, the educated Jews of the town, could provide a sympathetic ear. "Excellent men with high ideals" was the group with whom Freud wanted to be identified. In the next part of the letter, Freud makes it clear that this was also a coded statement referring to the *Jewish* nature of the B'nai Brith, and that this mattered greatly to him:

> That you were Jews could only be welcome to me, for I was myself a Jew, and it has always appeared to me not only undignified, but outright foolish to deny it. What tied me to Jewry was—I have to admit it—not the faith, not even the national pride, for I was always an unbeliever, have been brought up without religion, but not without respect for the so-called "ethical" demands of human civilisation. Whenever I have experienced feelings of national exaltation, I have tried to suppress them as disastrous and unfair, frightened by the warning example of those nations among which we Jews live. But there remained enough to make the attraction of Judaism and the Jews irresistible, many

> dark emotional powers all the stronger the less they could be expressed in words, as well as the clear consciousness of an inner identity, the familiarity of the same psychological structure. And before long there followed the realisation that it was only to my Jewish nature that I owed the two qualities that have become indispensable to me throughout my difficult life. Because I was a Jew, I found myself free of many prejudices which restrict others in the use of the intellect; as a Jew I was prepared to be in the opposition and to renounce agreement with the "compact majority."[8]

This letter has elicited many comments on its implication that antisemitism strengthens the ability of the Jew to face a life of opposition, as well as Freud's very interesting remarks on how Jewish identity does not depend on shared religious or national beliefs but is somehow more "emotional." These issues have been central to many studies of Freud's Jewishness, which at the very least have established how important this identity was to him, whatever his thoroughly atheistic and non-Zionist credentials. In relation to the writing of *The Interpretation of Dreams*, it is also noteworthy that the context in which Freud could report on his self-analysis and reveal so much personal material was an accepting, Jewish one. This once again feeds into a conceptualization of psychoanalysis as emerging from a very specific position: Freud's personality and his location in the Jewish world of Vienna, after the death of his father. Many have argued that coupled with the restricted base of Freud's patients—at first mostly bourgeois Jews in Vienna; later many international visitors, usually intellectuals attracted to psychoanalysis and possibly to practicing it—this means that psychoanalysis cannot claim to have made universal discoveries applicable to all people. There is truth in this argument, but we could also say that the acknowledgment of the specificity of psychoanalysis' origins challenges us to think about how its model might apply elsewhere.

There is another thing to note about the resonance of this book for modern times. All of his own dreams reported by Freud in the first edition were dreamt during the closing years of the nineteenth century, during a period of personal and professional struggle for Freud in which he had to deal with his father's death, the needs of his growing young family, and his difficult, marginal position in the Viennese medical world. Out of this struggle, a new theory and method of psychological treatment emerged, which was full of excitement but also scandalous, particularly because of its obsession with sexuality but also through its assertion of the central role of irrational, unconscious impulses in human affairs. As such, these dreams and their interpretation can be seen as a kind of commentary not only on the situation in which Freud perceived himself to be, but also on the forces and social experiences that gave rise to the great modernist movements of the early twentieth century. These forces are most accurately characterized as "revolutionary." Images of volcanic upheaval, of the destruction of the outworn fabric of centuries by a new, exciting yet dangerous energy, are to be found in politics and in many cultural representations (literature, music, art) during this and the subsequent historical period. They are also to be found in Freud's thought. He admitted to having wanted to head the chapter on therapy in *The Interpretation of Dreams* with the caption "Flavit et dissipati sunt"—"He blew and they were scattered."[9] Whether this refers to the problems inherent in his clinical and theoretical work, to his opponents, or to the whole established order of things, the imagery here is that of revolution.

"Sexuality of Dreams"

There is a further peculiarity of *The Interpretation of Dreams* that is worth noting. We are used to thinking of Freudian dream analysis as being obsessed by sexuality, and this is a fair comment. As will be discussed more fully in the next chapter, sexuality and the sexual "drives" are very much at the center of Freud's early thinking, and sexual explanations of dreams are frequent in the book. However, in Freud's own dreams, there was more emphasis on self-justification, commonly aimed at legitimizing himself in relation to his father, even if there was often a screen of other people—colleagues and opponents—in the foreground. It is a psychoanalytic platitude that dreams of rivalry and triumph can be read Oedipally as victory over the father, and such dreams pervade the text with extraordinary regularity and ferocity. "Uncle Josef with the Yellow Beard" had Freud denigrating a friend in order to find a way of surpassing him professionally; the "Botanical Monograph" "turns out to have been in the nature of a self-justification, a plea on behalf of my own rights."[10] In his analysis of the "Count Thun" dream, Freud disavowed the significance of his paternity, identifying the dream thought as "It is absurd to be proud of one's ancestry; it is better to be an ancestor oneself."[11] As described in Chapter 2, Freud recollected his father's prediction that he would "come to nothing" and showed how his dream represented a triumph over it—not just proving the father wrong, but humiliating him as well. Most explicitly, in the context of the "Rome" dreams, Freud recalled his father's passivity in the face of antisemitic abuse and contrasted it with his own heroic identifications—although, as French psychoanalyst Didier Anzieu points out, all the heroes documented by Freud in the commentary on the dream eventually failed to achieve their aspirations.[12]

The best-known dream of the book is another one of Freud's, the famous "specimen dream" of "Irma's injection." This dream has a whole chapter dedicated to it and is presented as an illustration of the method of dream interpretation, which largely consists of breaking the dream up into its components and analyzing each of these separately. Freud was immensely proud of the dream and of his work on it; a footnote at the end of the dream inserted by the editors of the Standard Edition of Freud's writings states, "In a letter to Fliess on June 12, 1900, Freud describes a later visit to Bellevue, the house where he had this dream. 'Do you suppose,' he writes, 'that some day a marble tablet will be placed on the house, inscribed with these words?—In This House, on July 24th, 1895, the Secret of Dreams was Revealed to Dr. Sigm. Freud. At the moment there seems little prospect of it.'"[13] Roudinesco notes that "Not until May 6, 1977, was Freud's wish granted and a plaque placed on the Bellevue house."[14] Not many people have a single dream commemorated in this way.

"Irma" was a pseudonym, probably a composite patient but with traces of Emma Eckstein who, as described in the previous chapter, was the victim of a scandalous piece of medical negligence on the part of Freud's friend Fliess. As was common in those early days, she was also a family friend of Freud's. In the "Preamble" to the dream, Freud writes that the dream was precipitated by a visit to his holiday home by a friend and colleague "Otto," who was staying with Irma's family at their country resort. Freud asked him how he had found her and he answered. "She's better, but not quite well."

> I was conscious that my friend Otto's words, or the tone in which he spoke them, annoyed me. I fancied I detected a reproof in them, such as to the effect that I had promised the patient too much; and, whether rightly or wrongly, I attributed the supposed fact of Otto's siding against me to the influence of my patient's relatives, who, as it seemed to me, had never looked with favour on the treatment. However, my disagreeable impression was not clear to me and I gave no outward sign of it. The same evening I wrote out Irma's case history, with the idea of giving it to Dr. M. (a common friend who was at that time the leading figure in our circle) in order to justify myself. That night (or more probably the next morning) I had the following dream, which I noted down immediately after waking.[15]

The dream is then described in detail. It is worth reproducing here as an example of how Freud's fantasy life permeated *The Interpretation of Dreams*, giving us a vivid sense of what he was imagining:

> *A large hall—numerous guests, whom we were receiving.—Among them was Irma. I at once took her on one side, as though to answer her letter and to reproach her for not having accepted my "solution" yet. I said to her: "If you still get pains, it's really only your fault." She replied: "If you only knew what pains I've got now in my throat and stomach and abdomen—it's choking me"—I was alarmed and looked at her. She looked pale and puffy. I thought to myself that after all I must be missing some organic trouble. I took her to the window and looked down her throat, and she showed signs of recalcitrance, like women with artificial dentures. I thought to myself that there was really no need for her to do that.—She then opened her mouth properly and on the right I found a big white patch; at another place I saw extensive whitish grey scabs upon some remarkable curly structures which were evidently modelled on the turbinal bones of the nose.—I at once called in Dr. M., and he repeated the examination and confirmed it. … Dr. M. looked quite different from usual; he was very pale, he walked with a limp and his chin was clean-shaven. … My friend Otto was now standing beside her as well, and my friend Leopold was percussing her through her bodice and saying: "She has a dull area low down on the left." He also indicated that a portion of the skin on the left shoulder was infiltrated. (I noticed this, just as he did, in spite of her dress.) … M. said: "There's no doubt it's an infection, but no matter; dysentery will supervene and the toxin will be eliminated." … We were directly aware, too, of the origin of the infection. Not long before, when she was feeling unwell, my friend Otto had given her an injection of a preparation of propyl, propyls … propionic acid … trimethylamin (and I saw before me the formula for this printed in heavy type) … Injections of that sort ought not to be made so thoughtlessly. … And probably the syringe had not been clean.*[16]

Given that Freud presents this dream as the key example of his art, it is perhaps surprising that he is very cautious about what he describes in his analysis. He says nothing about Fliess's mistreatment of Emma, although he does recollect an earlier occasion when a patient of his had died, and also the extremely painful episode of the death of Fleischl von Marxow after Freud had prescribed him cocaine. But despite these admissions and the presence of several sexual associations to the dream, Freud steps back from a full analysis and acknowledges that he has not provided all the information available to him. His conclusion, nevertheless, is a powerful one, which also summarizes Freud's theory of what dreams are about: "The dream acquitted me of the responsibility for Irma's condition by showing that it was due to other factors—it produced a whole series of reasons. The dream represented a particular state of affairs as I should have wished it to be. Thus its content was the fulfillment of a wish and its motive was a wish."[17] And then Freud offers a characteristic, famous, and very funny acknowledgment of just how hard he had to work to escape the criticism that he might not have been offering Irma the right treatment. Having listed all the contradictory ways in which the dream might relieve him of the blame for Irma's continued suffering (Irma's pains were organic, not psychological; they were due to the sexual frustration of widowhood; they had been caused by the injection), he comments, "The whole plea—for the dream was nothing else—reminded one vividly of the defence put forward by the man who was charged by one of his neighbours with having given him back a borrowed kettle in a damaged condition. The defendant asserted first, that he had given it back undamaged; secondly, that the kettle had a hole in it when he borrowed it; and thirdly, that he had never borrowed a kettle from his neighbour at all. So much the better: if only a single one of these three lines of defence were to be accepted as valid, the man would have to be acquitted."[18]

By his careful ordering and editing of the material in this dream report, Freud allows the dream to speak more by the centrality granted it—and by the evocativeness of the dream imagery itself—than by the comprehensiveness of the analysis. He admits suppressing revealing personal sexual material, nevertheless allowing the sexuality of the dream imagery to emerge clearly in the interpretation, thus preserving the energy and disturbance of the dream. Freud recollects "other medical examinations and … little secrets revealed in the course of them—to the satisfaction of neither party"; he thinks of Irma's "intimate woman friend," recalling that "I had often played with the idea that she too might ask me to relieve her of her symptoms," but "she was recalcitrant;" the friend would have yielded sooner. She would then "have opened her mouth properly."[19] Exploring the element in the dream in which an infected area on Irma's shoulder is noticed "in spite of her dress," Freud comments, "Frankly, I had no desire to penetrate more deeply at this point."[20] And, finally, there is Freud's reference to Fliess's theory about "some very remarkable connections between the turbinal bones and the female organs of sex."[21] Whatever other elements are present in the dream analysis, Freud allows it to speak in the barely coded language of sexuality.

The sexuality of dreams emerges very clearly in another famous text of Freud's published a few years after *The Interpretation of Dreams*, but meant as a companion piece to it, a living demonstration of the value of dream interpretation in work with neurotic patients, as well as an illustration of the correctness of his dream theory. This is *An Analysis of a Fragment of a Case of Hysteria*, better known as the "Dora" case study after its pseudonymous heroine.[22] "Dora" was Freud's first full-length case history, rich in literary and psychological complexity. Freud made it carry the burden of additional claims about the importance of sexuality in development and in neurosis. This includes advocating for the therapeutic potential of psychoanalysis and making a case for the ubiquity of homosexuality in neurosis. He also suggested that sexual "perversions" are, in a developmental sense, "normal" and he began to unravel the importance of the transference, which would become increasingly central to the theory and practice of psychoanalysis as the discipline developed. For these reasons, as well as for the sheer brilliance of the case history as a narrative—a "novella," as literary critic Steven Marcus calls it—"Dora" has been an extraordinarily seminal document in psychoanalysis.[23] This is not just because of its status as the first great case history, but also because it touched on numerous themes which have become contentious but productive in the history of psychoanalysis. In many respects, these themes center on the question of the status of psychoanalytic knowledge, or "mastery": what does the analyst know, and what does he (in this case) construct as a product of his own wishes and impulses?

The "Dora" Case Study

Dora was the name given by Freud to his young patient Ida Bauer—an interesting choice in its own right. In his 1901 book, *The Psychopathology of Everyday Life*, which was in fact written contemporaneously with the "Dora" case study, Freud discussed why this name came to mind:

> I asked myself how it was determined. Who else was there called Dora? I should have liked to dismiss with incredulity the next thought to occur to me—that it was the name of my sister's nursemaid; but I have so much self-discipline or so much practice in analysing that I held firmly to the idea and let my thoughts run on from it. At once there came to my mind a trivial incident from the previous evening which provided the determinant I was looking for. I had seen a letter on my sister's dining-room table addressed to "Fräulein Rosa W." I asked in surprise who there was of that name, and was told that the girl I knew as Dora was really

> called Rosa, but had had to give up her real name when she took up employment in the house, since my sister could take the name "Rosa" as applying to herself as well. "Poor people," I remarked in pity, "they cannot even keep their own names!" After that, I now recall, I fell silent for a moment and began to think of a variety of serious matters which drifted into obscurity, but which I was now easily able to make conscious. When next day I was looking for a name for someone who could not keep her own, "Dora" was the only one to occur to me. The complete absence of alternatives was here based on a solid association connected with the subject-matter that I was dealing with: for it was a person employed in someone else's house, a governess, who exercised a decisive influence on my patient's story, and on the course of the treatment as well.[24]

The Psychopathology of Everyday Life deals brilliantly with how the unconscious infiltrates mundane activities, and it contains many examples of errors, forgotten or misremembered statements, and the famous "Freudian slips." Along with another text from the same period, *Jokes and Their Relation to the Unconscious*, as well as *The Interpretation of Dreams*, this book showed in an easily accessible way how the apparently exotic claims of psychoanalysis, with its complex vocabulary and subtle ways of exploring hidden recesses of the mind, could be translated into everyday observations of a familiar and "normal" kind. Freud's account of how he chose the name for Ida/Dora is an example of this, even though it does not fit simply into the categories of jokes or slips of the tongue. It shows in action his belief that everything has a meaning, and this meaning is located in unconscious thought processes. Ida became Dora because Rosa/Dora lost her name—because she was a governess, like one of the central figures in the "Dora" case and because Freud sought some kind of revenge on Dora for the way *she* treated *him*.

When Dora saw Freud in 1899, she was eighteen years old and had been suffering from a variety of troubling symptoms—depression, coughing, and loss of voice, along with suicidal tendencies. Indeed, the trigger for her father taking her to Freud was the discovery of a suicide note. The real reason, however, as Freud was quick to work out, was that Dora was aware of an affair between her father and a family friend, "Frau K." The father was hoping that Freud would make Dora see sense—which meant, stop objecting to the affair. The pernicious sexual economy of this was that Dora's father had apparently encouraged a liaison between Dora and Herr K., his lover's husband; but Dora had "hysterically" rejected him. The text of "Dora" is a complicated one, showing some of Freud's prejudices in a way that has made him, to this day, the target of criticism from many feminists. But it also demonstrates the seriousness with which he took women's sexual desires and a kind of intrepid refusal to abet manipulations by Dora's father. What mattered to him was to understand why Dora might have reacted "neurotically" to the situation; the fact that the situation was real—that she was right in her estimation of what was going on—did not change this concern. In its pure "Freudian" form, psychoanalysis is not so much interested in the situation people find themselves in—which is always likely to be troublesome and will often be disastrous—but, rather, in what that situation means to them and what disturbance it provokes. This has at times led to a neglect of external circumstances that are provoking a person's difficulties, a critical point that has often been important for those wanting to use psychoanalysis to address social factors such as racism and sexism.

The main agenda of "Dora," however, was for Freud to show that interpretation of dreams could add to the understanding of neurosis and help work with it. He did this through the analysis of two dreams brought to him by Dora. The first dream was seemingly a simple one:

> *A house was on fire. My father was standing beside my bed and woke me up. I dressed quickly. Mother wanted to stop and save her jewel-case; but Father said: "I refuse to let myself and my two children be*

> *burnt for the sake of your jewel-case." We hurried downstairs, and as soon as I was outside I woke up.*[25]

The analysis of this dream is presented by Freud as a kind of screenplay in which there is a lively dialogue between him and his young patient, tracking her associations and his suggestions and interpretations until a final denouement is reached. This focuses on masturbation. Freud finds a clue to Dora's practice in a "symptomatic act" of hers within the consulting room. Immediately after Freud suggested she masturbated in childhood, Dora turned up with a "reticule" (a small handbag) and spent much of the session opening and closing it. Freud's interpretation is direct and scandalous:

> Dora's reticule, which came apart at the top in the usual way, was nothing but a representation of the genitals, and her playing with it, her opening it and putting her finger in it, was an entirely unembarrassed yet unmistakable pantomimic announcement of what she would like to do with them—namely, to masturbate.[26]

And then Freud shows his affinity with another great figure of the same period, albeit a fictional one, Sherlock Holmes:

> There is a great deal of symbolism of this kind in life, but as a rule we pass it by without heeding it. When I set myself the task of bringing to light what human beings keep hidden within them, not by the compelling power of hypnosis, but by observing what they say and what they show, I thought the task was a harder one than it really is. He that has eyes to see and ears to hear may convince himself that no mortal can keep a secret.[27]

There is, of course, a great deal more in Freud's analysis of this dream and of its companion piece, in which Dora is told by her mother that her father has died and then struggles to find her way to the funeral. Again, Freud provides a sexual interpretation, relating to Dora's hidden knowledge of sexual acts. In the analysis of both dreams, there are many Oedipal themes that connect with Dora's love for her father, and a homosexual sub-text involving both her governess (the source of her sexual knowledge) and Frau K. All this was carried out with great aplomb, but it did not stop Dora from abandoning the treatment, though she seemed to have derived some benefit from it. Roudinesco reports, using the real names for Dora, Frau K., and Herr K., that "Ida never got over her rejection of men. But her symptoms decreased. After her short analysis, she got her revenge for the humiliation she had suffered by making Peppina admit her liaison and Hans admit his attempt at seduction. She then reported the truth to her father, and broke off all relations with the couple. In 1903 she married Ernst Adler, a composer employed in her father's factory. Two years later she gave birth to a son who eventually had a career as a musician in the United States."[28] This is all true, but it is also worth noting a vicious and vindictive appraisal of Ida by the analyst Felix Deutsch, who met her several years later, in 1923. In his report, he includes a comment by an "informant" that Ida was "one of the most repulsive hysterics he had ever met."[29]

"Dora" is not set up as a test of psychoanalysis' power as a treatment, but as an account of how to interpret dreams, and a demonstration of their place in psychoanalytic therapy. It is not often read that way but, as such, it reveals how Freud came into his own as a startling magician both of the unconscious and of literary style. He brings his patient and himself to life in this account. Indeed, he goes out of his way in his Preface to denounce "physicians who (revolting though it may seem) choose to read a case history of this kind not as a contribution to the psycho-pathology of the neuroses, but as a roman à clef designed for their private delectation," precisely because the case history reads like a novel. The dreams give a strong sense of Dora/Ida's interior world, and their analysis gives an even more compelling evocation of the relationship between doctor and patient as two "subjects"—people with their own inner lives—trying to make sense of the complicated situation in which they find themselves.

And this is really where we have arrived at with this account of the two dream books, *The Interpretation of Dreams* and the *Fragment of an Analysis*. Freud was up and running as the first psychoanalyst. He was a scientist, for sure, but a very peculiar one: a scientist who was willing to get involved in the most hidden elements of psychic life and to argue it through with his patients, with his readers, and with the whole hypocritical society in which he lived.

4

Sexuality

Freud did not exactly invent sex, but he did have a lot to do with its popularization. Or rather, he developed an understanding of sex and sexuality that was much broader than most people previously held. He "normalized" sexual behavior in the sense of demonstrating that practices often deemed aberrant were, in fact, part of many people's sexual repertoire. He encouraged an understanding of sexuality as central to people's psychological as well as physical life. He developed a complex account of the unconscious dynamics of sexual desire that has often been challenged and disdained, but which has proved to be a firm foundation for liberalizing attitudes and for sexual expressiveness.

Freud did not do this alone. In the late nineteenth century, there was an enormous amount of scientific activity about sex, as well as some scathingly astute political and artistic exposés of sexual hypocrisy. Medical doctors, psychiatrists, and sexologists juggled with varying understandings of sex, with heredity and masturbation being at the center of speculations on the causes and (to a lesser extent) cures of sexual pathology. Freud came into this morass as a researcher interested in the sources of hysteria and obsessional neurosis, and as a clinician faced with actual hysterics and other neurotics who he was meant to help. His approach eventually offered an accepting "voice" to sexual desires, maybe especially for women. And all this, perhaps oddly, from a man whose own sexuality seems to have been highly constrained, limited to a few years of early married life in which six children were born. As noted earlier, he may also have had an affair with his sister-in-law Minna Bernays, who lived with the Freud family for most of her life—though while some commentators are totally convinced that such an affair took place, tracing it in particular to holidays taken with Minna in the late 1890s, others, such as Elisabeth Roudinesco, are dubious about the loose ends and slight straws that constitute the actual evidence.[1] Whatever the case, for the second half of his life Freud probably had little or no sex, even though his writings were full of it. Perhaps this can be seen as some evidence for his own concept of *sublimation*—the idea that sexual drives can be converted into socially valued cultural forms; work instead of sex!

Sex did, in fact, cause quite a few problems for Freudian theory. In the mid-1890s, he was struggling to answer the question of what caused neuroses, particularly hysteria, and was resistant to the idea that it was simply hereditary. From his clinical work and the material covered in *Studies on Hysteria* and other places, he became convinced that there was an environmental, traumatic origin to neurosis. The source that kept returning is what is now known as child sexual abuse, or in his time as "sexual seduction" or "molestation" of children by adults. Makari puts this claim in context, referring to a letter from Freud to Fliess on the first day of 1896:

> On January 1, 1896, Freud spelled out his thinking: hysteria was caused by sexual molestation during childhood. The sexual molestation of children was not unknown among nineteenth century forensic physicians. … However, Freud was not just saying that molested children became hysterical. He claimed that childhood molestations quietly festered for years before causing adult hysteria. Like syphilis, this latent disruption broke out in mental illness only later in life. Freud reasoned that the event remained quiescent and only gathered pathogenic force with the emergence of mature sexuality. Only then would the memories of sexual molestation take on meaning, provoke horror, and engender repression.[2]

The idea that being subjected to sexual abuse in childhood might cause psychological difficulties in adulthood was not especially radical then, any more than it is now. Where Freud's account differed, however, was that he made sexual abuse the cause of *all* neuroses, with the differing symptoms of various neurotic disorders being a function of the age at which the molestation had taken place. Moreover, Freud's claim went further, right to the heart of middle-European "Victorian" society. Makari comments that "Freud now concluded that sexual molestations were perpetrated not by bad governesses, older children, and strangers, but always by the child's father. While cases of paternal sexual abuse had been documented, Freud's belief that the father was the culprit in all cases of psychoneurosis simply had no precedent."[3] This belief caused much opposition in the professional circles in which Freud wished to move; and eventually, it caused difficulties for him as well. Not only was the evidence that every single neurotic had been abused by their father lacking (as such evidence is always likely to be, given that it takes only one "negative" case to make the theory untenable), but it also presented Freud with a dilemma in himself. He knew that he had plenty of neurotic traits, including psychosomatic symptoms and an addictive personality, yet while he was at first willing to countenance the possibility that his own father had sexually abused him, this was not a convincing accusation and was at variance both with what he knew of his father's personality and with what was being generated in his emerging self-analysis.

By the summer of 1897, Freud was wavering in his belief in the ubiquity of sexual abuse. After a holiday in Italy, he returned to Vienna and took what is often seen as the "brave" (but, in fact, necessary) step of renouncing his previous theory—the theory that he had hoped would bring him fame and fortune. Freud evokes this turning point, another one of those moments that could be claimed as an origin for psychoanalysis proper, in a letter to Fleiss of September 21, 1897. This letter has become very famous and is worth quoting at some length:

> And now I want to confide in you immediately the great secret that has been slowly dawning on me in the last few months. I no longer believe in my *neurotica*. This is probably not intelligible without an explanation; after all, you yourself found credible what I was able to tell you. So I will begin historically [and tell you] where the reasons for disbelief came from. The continual disappointment in my efforts to bring a single analysis to a real conclusion; the running away of people who for a period of time had been most gripped [by analysis]; the absence of the complete successes on which I had counted; the possibility of explaining to myself the partial successes in other ways, in the usual fashion—this was the first group. Then the surprise that in all cases, the father, not excluding my own, had to be accused of being perverse—the realization of the unexpected frequency of hysteria, with precisely the same conditions prevailing in each, whereas surely such widespread perversions against children are not very probable. The [incidence] of perversion would have to be immeasurably more frequent than the [resulting] hysteria because the illness, after all, occurs only where there has been an accumulation of events and there is a contributory factor that weakens the defense. Then, third, the certain insight that there are no indications of reality in the unconscious, so that one cannot distinguish between truth and fiction that has been cathected with affect … If I were depressed, confused, exhausted, such doubts would surely have to be interpreted as signs of weakness. Since I am in an opposite state, I must recognize them as the result of honest and vigorous intellectual work and must be proud that after going so deep I am still capable of such criticism. Can it be that this doubt merely represents an episode in the advance toward further insight?[4]

The last section of this quotation is part of the evidence employed by people who argue that one of Freud's most striking characteristics was his ability to remain open to new ideas, to see where his theories did not stand up to scrutiny, and to adjust them in the light of new experience. There is much truth in this claim, though it is also possible to see it as a way of justifying himself, a defense against the depression to which he was prone, especially in light of the embarrassment over the demolition of his theoretical edifice. This is indeed supported by a slightly later passage in the same letter:

> The expectation of eternal fame was so beautiful, as was that of certain wealth, complete independence, travels, and lifting the children above the severe worries that robbed me of my youth. Everything depended upon whether or not hysteria would come out right. Now I can once again remain quiet and modest, go on worrying and saving. A little story from my collection occurs to me: "Rebecca, take off your gown; you are no longer a bride." In spite of all this, I am in very good spirits and content that you feel a need to see me again similar to mine to see you.[5]

Freud seems to be struggling here, and understandably so, to maintain his equilibrium.

The quotation makes clear what the intellectual grounds were for Freud's repudiation of his "seduction theory," as it has come to be known. First, it was no help to him in analysis with his patients. Given that Freud believed that revealing the truth of trauma—that is, establishing the actual events that lay at the source of a psychological disturbance—would remove the disturbance itself, the failure to be therapeutically successful suggested that he was looking in the wrong places. This issue of the relationship between psychoanalytic truth and therapeutic improvement has continued to dog psychoanalysis to the present day. Second, sexual abuse might have been widespread in society then, as now, but the implication that it was pretty much universal was clearly untenable. Both these are important points, but in some ways, the third one (Freud also lists a fourth reason, to do with psychosis) is the most significant for what was to come next. Freud notes "the certain insight that there are no indications of reality in the unconscious, so that one cannot distinguish between truth and fiction that has been cathected with affect." This passage suggests that Freud was already alert to how unconscious thought processes are flooded with fantasy, making it impossible to distinguish reliably between an actual recollection and a wish. This is both a problematic and a revolutionary claim. It is problematic because it questions the truth status of statements about what has happened. As such, it lays psychoanalysis open to the criticism that it treats memories of real events as fantasies, thus failing to take accusations of mistreatment and abuse seriously. This has been, rightly, a major source of dissent with traditional psychoanalysis, especially from feminists and radical critics. The abandonment of the seduction theory also moved Freud's approach away from a focus on the traumatic origin of mental suffering, and toward a more "constitutional," or at least "internal" focus. In this, what matters is not so much what has happened to people, but how they *experience* it and respond to it. This move has considerable explanatory power, answering questions such as why two people who have the same traumatic experience might respond quite differently. It also tends to make Freudian theory under-appreciative of the impact of external events, and more focused on the attributes of individuals that determine how they respond to these occurrences.

On the other hand, Freud's revitalized focus on fantasy is perhaps what defines psychoanalysis' special contribution. No longer is the situation one of "environment" versus "heredity" in the crude way that continues to be espoused by many commentators. Freud suggests that whatever happened—and he certainly did not underplay the importance of trauma, including sexual abuse, in his post-1897 work—is felt by individuals in relation to their "unconscious" mental life. Something horrific will affect a person; but the nature of that impact will depend on how it becomes part of that person's "psychic reality." To understand this, we need to have an intimate and complex knowledge of their fantasy life. This is a revolutionary idea, because it breaks down the distinction between "inner" and "outer" worlds; we are always in transition between them. It also has some political connotations which do not necessarily run in the direction that might be expected by the many authors who have criticized Freud for abandoning the seduction theory and supposedly underplaying the importance of child sexual abuse. Roudinesco puts it like this:

> By giving up the idea that the bourgeois family order could be based on the alliance between a perverse parent and an abused child, Freud … was leaving the realm of describing behaviours for that of interpreting discourse, considering that the famous sexual scenes described by patients could stem from fantasies, that is, from subjective or imaginary representations. And he added that even when an instance of seduction had actually occurred, it was not necessarily the source of a neurosis. Thus he accepted simultaneously the existence of fantasy and that of trauma.[6]

The goal of this approach is not to reduce the power of trauma but to show how it works psychologically to disturb the process of development.

The Importance of the Three Essays

Freud's most important text on sexuality, *Three Essays on the Theory of Sexuality*, was published eight years after his 1897 letter, and revised several times over the next twenty years. By this point, he was well past sorrowing over his abandonment of the seduction theory, and had in his possession an extraordinary range of ideas that would organize the psychoanalytic vision of sexuality for decades to come. One issue of note in the shift from "seduction" to the psychoanalytically more mature account given in the *Three Essays* is that seduction makes the infant relatively passive. Something is done to the child, and this act distorts and damages their sexual development and later well-being. While the new theory did not dismiss the reality of sexual abuse, the focus was very different. The new claim is that the infant is a sexual being from the start of life. What we see in development is the gradual organization of this sexuality into more or less recognizable "adult" forms, without ever completely diminishing the continued presence of the basic elements of infantile sexuality itself. All those aspects of sexual life that seemed "pathological" to writers in Freud's time—and, still, to many people in our time too—can be understood as enactments of, or "fixations" upon, organizations of sexuality characteristic of the period of early development.

Children, then, are not asexual innocents rudely awakened into sexual life by the abusive interference of adults, or indeed simply by the biologically normal emergence of sexual characteristics in puberty. They are *always* sexual, and the difficulty is that society hypocritically refuses to acknowledge this fact. Sexuality is also the fundamental driving force behind psychic life. Sexual energy and sexual drive are the source of human behavior and unconscious conflict. Sexuality is biologically rooted, but it does not *reduce* to biology. That is, the sexual drive is somehow *excessive*, more than is needed simply to keep the species going. Sexuality, according to psychoanalysis, works in the service of pleasure rather than of reproduction; that is one reason it can be seen as a characteristic of childhood—well before reproduction comes into the picture. Looking back on his work in later life (in his 1920 text *Beyond the Pleasure Principle*), Freud argued that this claim was one reason for opposition to psychoanalysis. It is true that psychoanalysis very quickly polarized people because of its commitment to the idea of sexual pleasure as the core of human striving, and its refusal to judge this as morally wrong. Freud writes,

> The concept of "sexuality," and at the same time of the sexual instinct, had, it is true, to be extended so as to cover many things

> which could not be classed under the reproductive function; and this caused no little hubbub in an austere, respectable or merely hypocritical world.[7]

Freud's opposition to sexual hypocrisy was an early way in which psychoanalysis committed itself to social critique, putting it at odds with social conventions although not necessarily with the escalating interest in sexuality that marked its time. It is also worth noting that despite Freud's self-presentation as scandalizing and isolated, the *Three Essays* was quite well-received at the time, and over the next twenty years was sufficiently successful as a publication to warrant three new editions.

Nevertheless, Freud was not wrong about the revolutionary status of the *Three Essays*. Makari describes its impact on reviewers as "astounding," succinctly explaining why.

> With lightning speed, the author took apart, reframed, and re-presented the major questions facing sexology. What made for sexual difference? What was inborn and what was the result of experience? What constituted normal sexual development? What kinds of sexual desires were abnormal? What was love? In three terse, tightly argued essays, Freud presented crushing critiques of prevailing theories of sexuality, and then lifted out of that rubble a synthesis centered on a theory of the sexual drive, which he called "libido."[8]

The three essays are titled "The Sexual Aberrations," "Infantile Sexuality," and "The Transformations of Puberty." Under these scientific-sounding titles (though of course, the middle one has its scandalous nature) are many subtle and sober arguments. The net effect is a significant reinvention of the relationship between so-called "normality" and sexuality. This makes sexual desire and the organization of the sexual drive central to human psychology, breaking down the opposition between normal and pathological—

especially between the normal and the "perverse"—that always seems to capture the imagination and energy of sexual conservatives. Partly this is because Freud shows that sexuality is at the core of not just the so-called perversions, but also of the neuroses, seen as a more acceptable set of disorders—more like illness than bad behavior. Neurotics simply repress their perverted desires; all of us are in any case perverted, because we all inherit the tendencies of a "polymorphously perverse" childhood.

Freud writes in the *Three Essays*:

> In view of what was now seen to be the wide dissemination of tendencies to perversion we were driven to the conclusion that a disposition to perversions is an original and universal disposition of the human sexual instinct and that normal sexual behaviour is developed out of it as a result of organic changes and psychical inhibitions occurring in the course of maturation.[9]

Adult sexuality arises from a number of components seen separately in childhood, and accumulated through a developmental sequence whereby sexual enjoyment is organized successively around different body parts. These are the "erogenous zones" of mouth, anus, and genitals, structured through the "oral," "anal," "phallic," and "genital" stages of sexual life. Fixation or regression to these stages, which constitutes both an inhibition of sexual development and recognition of their persistence in adult life, is the source of neurosis and perversion. But the more important point is that there is continuity between the sexual life of the child and that of the adult. Freud reasons:

> It appeared [that] the sexual instinct itself must be something put together from various factors, and that in the perversions it falls apart, as it were, into its components. The perversions were thus seen to be on the one hand inhibitions, and on the other hand dissociations, of normal development. Both these aspects were brought together in the supposition that the sexual instinct

> of adults arises from a combination of a number of impulses of childhood into a unity, an impulsion with a single aim.[10]

One of the difficulties encountered when reading the *Three Essays* is that in the various new editions Freud offered many important elaborations of his ideas without changing the main text. The result is a wonderfully "modernist" book, in which there is a core narrative (the 1905 version) and what author Steven Marcus, referring to the "Dora" case but equally applicable here, called "those stop-you-dead-in-your-tracks footnotes that he was so expert in using strategically."[11] Some of these refer to the notion of the Oedipus complex. This had long been in Freud's armory, since he commented to Fliess in 1897 that the continuing power of Sophocles's play *Oedipus Rex* was due to how "the Greek legend seizes on a compulsion which everyone recognizes because he feels its existence within himself. Each member of the audience was once, in germ and in phantasy, just such an Oedipus."[12] What does this mean? "I have found, in my own case too, falling in love with the mother and jealousy of the father, and I now regard it as a universal event of early childhood," Freud told Fliess.[13] From here, the Oedipus "complex" emerged in Freud's thinking, and even though he did not name it as such until 1910, it appeared in the 1915 footnotes to the *Three Essays* and remains indissolubly associated with them.

The Oedipus Complex, Femininity, and Homosexuality

The Oedipus complex is a slightly—though not very!—more complicated notion than the standard presentation of it in popular culture (for instance, "Oedipus, Schmoedipus—he's just a boy who loves his mother"). Freud's understanding of human psychology was that it was underpinned by biological drives, the most important of which is the sexual drive. Early sexuality, understood as the search for pleasurable release of the tension created by the drive, is expressed through oral impulses. These gradually are joined by, and partly give way to, anal impulses and then phallic and genital ones. What this means psychologically is not only that different parts of the body give pleasure, but also that different aspects of sexuality come to the fore as "characteristics." For example, the oral phase of biting and sucking has a great deal of aggression in it that can become preserved across life as an inclination to sarcasm and bitterness. The anal phase is more focused on the dynamic between giving and hoarding, though it has its own aggressive elements too. Phallic sexuality is thrusting and also possessive, but it has another characteristic that is even more important. In the oral and anal stages, infants are understood to direct their impulses toward "part objects," basically fantasies generated by early engagements with the outside environment, particularly the maternal breast. By the time the phallic stage is entered, at around three years of age, the child is more capable of integrating these experiences into gradually emerging "whole objects"—the mother and the father. The breast remains an object of desire, but it is now experienced as part of the mother; the phallus may be a threat that is bound up with the father.

This leads to the Oedipal situation. In the boy's case, his desire is for the mother, but he is also aware of the fact that the father stands in the way of his passion, and that the father is far more powerful than he is. Freud argued that there is no reason why the child should not desire the mother—she is, after all, the main source of his sexual satisfaction (oral and anal) to date. Therefore, the child is "naturally" incestuous in his desires. From the social world, however, epitomized in the family relationships in which the boy is embedded ("mummy-daddy-me"), this desire is untenable and immoral. For what is effectively the first time, the social world, in the person of the father, consequently says, "No: you may go this far and no further; this wish cannot be fulfilled." The child's "natural" incestuous desire, operating without consideration of the conventions that determine what is or is not an acceptable sexual object, is opposed by a "non-natural" but universal incest taboo, which structures this desire into a socialized form. This operates through a threat, experienced by the boy as a potential attack by the powerful father on the aspect of the child that is motivating his revolt. What is this aspect? Clearly, it is his sexuality, now focused on his penis. Hence the boy experiences a threat to his sexual potency, and this is known as the "castration complex."

The boy is overwhelmed by the castration complex, and matters are made worse by the way his own aggression against the father (whom he also loves) is defended against by use of projection—that is, it is pushed out of the child, who cannot bear it, and into the father. In this way, the father becomes even more threatening. Not only is he believed by the child to be hostile toward him because of the child's rivalrous desire for the mother, but he also contains the child's own projected hostile fantasies. There is no way that the feeble boy can stand up to this level of fantasized aggression from the powerful adult man, so instead, he uses a strategy of appeasement to make things all right. Psychoanalytically, this appeasement works in two ways. First, the child's desire for his mother becomes *repressed*, which means that the child does not give it up, but it is "relegated" to unconscious status, and denied access to awareness. Second, the boy *identifies* with his father. This puts them on the "same side," meaning that the boy can hold onto the idea that he could eventually take his father's place in a more orderly, acceptable way—for instance, by finding a wife whose status in respect to him would be the same as his mother's in relation to the father. He thus has some compensation for giving up his desire: at some point, sexual power and authority will be his.

Clearly, this account is a strongly "masculinist" one. Freud did not really consider the origins and nature of feminine sexuality until the mid-1920s (there is only a short section on it in the *Three Essays*), and while he worried about it for many years, he never developed a satisfactory account. It is worth raising an eyebrow here. After all, most of Freud's early patients were women, so it is probably a sign of the times as well as of his own blind spots around femininity—blind spots which sometimes drifted into anti-feminist rhetoric and misogyny—that he did not give it serious consideration when laying down the foundations of his sexual theory. When Freud did return to consider feminine sexuality, he did not do much better. This was something he seemed to recognize himself: for instance, at the end of his *New Introductory Lecture* on femininity, he commented, "That is all I had to say to you about femininity. It is certainly incomplete and fragmentary and does not always sound friendly."[14] He was right.

When considering feminine sexuality, Freud saw girls as facing the same issues as boys, but managing them in different ways, largely because of differences in the anatomy of the two genders and the different psychological complexes to which this gives rise. The male and the female child both have to come to terms with the structuring power of the father's authority and to give up their desire for the first object of infantile love, the mother. Both genders are active in their initial sexual activity so that "We are now obliged to recognize that the little girl is a little man."[15] But when it comes to the phallic stage of development, the boy centers his sexual life on the penis, while the girl's leading erotic zone is the clitoris. This has consequences that many commentators have seen as a sign of Freud's patriarchal neurosis rather than his scientific acuity.

According to Freud, the little girl, dependent on her clitoris for sexual stimulation, becomes aware of how small it is in comparison to the boy's penis. She assumes that because of this difference in size, it must also be *inferior* as an organ, an assumption which does not actually seem necessary, but which Freud and many other analysts have thought must be so. This leads the girl to experience a mixture of impassioned and negative emotions. She gains a general sense of her own inferiority in the world linked with the relative ineffectiveness of her genitals in providing satisfaction for the sexual drive; she feels rage at the mother for having created her like that; and she develops a passionate envy of the real thing, the penis possessed by father and brother alike. The little girl, just like the boy, wishes for a penis the size of the father's, and therefore wants to become like him and to displace him. But she cannot "have" the penis in this way, she realizes, because of the in-built difference, so she cannot model her future on identification with the father. Instead, her identification becomes an ambivalent one. She despises the mother for being insufficient and hates her for having made her the same; but she also both identifies and competes with her in wanting the father for herself, in wanting to take her place and be desirable in a world of men.

One thing to notice about Freud's theory here is that it reverses the account of the boy's development, although not in a completely symmetrical fashion. The boy's castration complex emerges *as a result of* the Oedipus complex: the boy first feels desire for the mother and rivalry with the father, and then fantasizes that he will be damaged by the father's aggression. The girl, however, first recognizes herself as "already castrated," having no penis, and because of this, she enters the Oedipus situation, in which her desire is to displace the mother to get for herself a share in the father's power. This is why, according to Freud, young girls feel strong unconscious hostility toward their mothers. It is also the source of the shift of sexual object from mother to father necessary for normative, heterosexual femininity. *Failures* of this Oedipal realignment of sexual desire can lead to lesbianism and/or neurosis. Finally, as Freud wrote in his *New Introductory Lecture* on feminine sexuality, the girl's desire for the penis must itself be renounced and replaced by the desire for a baby, "in accordance with an ancient symbolic equivalence." Freud suggested that the mother's happiness "is great if later on this wish for a baby finds fulfillment in reality and quite especially so if the baby is a little boy who brings the longed-for penis with him."[16]

Even this brief outline of Freud's theory of feminine sexuality will make it obvious why he was opposed by the feminist psychoanalysts of the 1920s and then again by second-wave feminists in the 1960s and 1970s. Since then, there has been a major realignment of the relationship between feminism and psychoanalysis, with the advent of some powerful feminist critics who have either been drawn to psychoanalysis or become psychoanalysts themselves. The most notable of these is Juliet Mitchell, who began this realignment. Her *Psychoanalysis and Feminism*, published in 1974, was a watershed text in rebranding Freudianism as a "theory of patriarchy" rather than just a patriarchal theory.[17] This book was extremely influential and provoked a genre of work along similar lines. In addition, post-Freudian developments in psychoanalysis that have made relationships more central and produced new theories of mothering have also helped bring about a reconceptualization of femininity and of sexual difference more generally. But back in Freud's day and in his work, this was all quite a mess—a matter of some chagrin, given that among the innovations for which Freud was responsible was acknowledgment that women's sexuality is active and real and that women, just as much as men, have sexual desires that need, and deserve, to be met.

Returning to the *Three Essays*, Freud did much better on another shibboleth, homosexuality. Here it is worth quoting a long footnote to the 1915 edition. This sheds light not just on his personal attitude, which was liberal about homosexuality, perhaps based on recognition of the "homoerotic" elements of his own personality, shown so clearly in his relationship with Fliess. It also conveys scientific considerations around bisexuality, the existence of what Freud called the "negative" Oedipus complex characterized by love for the parent of the *same* sex and jealous hatred of the parent of the opposite sex, and the nature of libido (sexual energy):

> Psychoanalytic research is most decidedly opposed to any attempt at separating off homosexuals from the rest of mankind as a group of a special character. By studying sexual excitations other than those that are manifestly displayed, it has found that all human beings

> are capable of making a homosexual object-choice and have in fact made one in their unconscious. Indeed, libidinal attachments to persons of the same sex play no less a part as factors in normal mental life, and a greater part as a motive force for illness, than do similar attachments to the opposite sex. On the contrary, psychoanalysis considers that a choice of an object independently of its sex—freedom to range equally over male and female objects—as it is found in childhood, in primitive states of society and early periods of history, is the original basis from which, as a result of restriction in one direction or the other, both the normal and the inverted types develop. Thus from the point of view of psychoanalysis the exclusive sexual interest felt by men for women is also a problem that needs elucidating and is not a self-evident fact based upon an attraction that is ultimately of a chemical nature. A person's final sexual attitude is not decided until after puberty and is the result of a number of factors, not all of which are yet known; some are of a constitutional nature but others are accidental.[18]

Freud goes on to discuss what "accidental" and experiential factors may make one sexual choice more likely than another, but the important point is clear. Homosexuality is a potential in everyone, and while the development of homosexuality in a person might be subject to psychoanalytic explanation, the same will be true of heterosexuality: "From the point of view of psychoanalysis the exclusive sexual interest felt by men for women is also a problem that needs elucidating." This is a genuinely emancipatory principle and much more progressive than was true for many later Freudians, for whom homosexuality represented a form of arrested development which, until the last couple of decades, was even an indication that a person should not train to be an analyst. Freud did not share this belief, and his antagonism to the pathologizing of homosexuality is clear in this example as it is in several other places.

By the end of 1905, Freud had published a series of texts that firmly established psychoanalysis as a new discipline, distinct from prevailing approaches to psychiatry and psychology. These major texts, *The Interpretation of Dreams*, *The Psychopathology of Everyday Life*, *Jokes and their Relation to the Unconscious*, *Three Essays on Sexuality*, and *Fragment of an Analysis of a Case of Hysteria*, testify to the workings of a creative and extraordinarily productive mind. They also remind us of his dependence on the domestic labor of the women supporting him, notably his wife Martha, but also his sister-in-law Minna, as well as a variety of maids and domestic workers whose assiduous childcaring, cooking, and cleaning freed the patriarch to work nonstop. But it has to be said that not every man who fails to help in the house (Freud seems never even to have gone shopping for groceries) produces so much radically significant work—written on top of a full clinical load, the earnings from which supported all his dependents. Whatever inhibitions Freud had, and however much he struggled with his neuroses, he freed himself from them sufficiently to create something new in this period of his life. In addition, he moved from being a contributor to a field with many competing voices to being a leader. And quite soon, this meant he had followers—not all of them to his liking, but enthusiasts nevertheless—who would begin the process, for better or worse, of turning Freudianism into a worldwide movement.

5

Founding a Movement

In 1902, after many years of waiting, with delays almost certainly due to antisemitism, Freud received the honorary title of "Professor" from the University of Vienna. This might have been one reason he felt emboldened to move out of his niche in the B'nai Brith and form his own society to discuss his new ideas. The new title was not due at that point to the overwhelming popularity of—or demand for—his thoughts. Judging by the sales figures of Freud's books, those who knew of his emerging theories and discoveries were a small band. By 1908, when the second edition of *The Interpretation of Dreams* was published, it had sold only six hundred copies, suggesting that the author's groundbreaking ideas were rather slow to take hold.

Nevertheless, the new discussion group, Freud's "Wednesday Society" as it was originally known, took hold, albeit from very modest beginnings. Its initial membership, besides Freud, was just four: Max Kahane, Wilhelm Stekel, Rudolf Reitler, and the man who was to become the first major schismatic in the psychoanalytic movement, Alfred Adler. The group expanded quickly to include others who were not necessarily doctors, for example, Max Graf, who was a musicologist and who later "treated" his own son under Freud's guidance, out of which came the famous "Little Hans" case study. This was important because it represented the "de-medicalizing" of psychoanalysis and its emergence into the wider culture. Indeed, in its early years, while Freud saw it as a scientific endeavor growing out of, and feeding back into, clinical work, much of its impetus came through its appeal to writers, artists, and musicians—what later would be called the "chattering classes" that gave end-of-the-century Vienna so much of its intellectual energy. The meetings themselves were very robust. Each one would be built around a talk by one of the members, most likely selected at random by drawing names from an urn (though it is not clear if this was the method for discussion after the formal talk, or for the talk itself). Roudinesco describes the scene: "During a short pause, they drank black coffee and ate delicious cakes. Then they plunged into interminable discussions, smoking cigars and cigarettes all the while. It was forbidden to read a paper written in advance, and no woman came in to disturb the banquet at which Freud was, in spite of himself, the secular prophet."[1] What happened, it seems, was a kind of free-for-all in which scientific and scholarly debate was mixed with personal material and often hostile attacks, with little sense of an organized group or an "orthodoxy" of views. Makari describes it as "a loose confederation of heretics."[2] Freud became discouraged watching and listening to his Viennese followers, a state of mind which had important consequences in terms of his later attitude to others who aligned themselves with him. Still, this was the first psychoanalytic organization, and it became the forerunner of an entire international movement.

Roudinesco's reference to smoking cigars and cigarettes "all the while" is not an accidental one. Smoking was an important element in the early life of the psychoanalytic movement, and it connected both with its gender politics (all the members of the Wednesday Society were men; women's smoking was much less socially acceptable) and with the addictive nature of psychoanalysis itself. In his entertaining and bitter history of the early analytic movement, written well after he had fallen out with Freud, Austrian physician and psychologist Wilhelm Stekel described the meetings of Freud's Wednesday Society in 1902 as completely engulfed in smoke and smoking:

> Freud initiated a specific ritual which continued for many years. We arrived there after the evening meal. There were cigars on the table to which most of the participants helped themselves generously. In

> the beginning, Freud smoked almost uninterruptedly. He smoked a small English pipe for which he had sacrificed his beloved Trabuko cigars, only to return to Trabukos again at a later stage. I have rarely seen a man smoke so much.[3]

Stekel was so impressed by all this that he wrote out the conversation about smoking that ensued and published it in a newspaper. He concluded this article with a short interchange on smoking as poison. Freud, it seems, denied that smoking was damaging—or denied it in relation to his own habit, which he claimed to be "moderate" (though Stekel noted how Freud's smoking was "uninterrupted"). Stekel himself introduced the idea of the last smoke ("tomorrow you'll quit"). This is, in fact, exactly the focus of the first great psychoanalytic novel, Italo Svevo's *Zeno's Conscience*, which centers on a man who cannot give up smoking, despite possessing a great capacity for free association, storytelling, and rationalization.[4] The last smoke apparently renounces pleasure while continuing to engage in it in an eternal present of unkept promises. In Stekel's version, Freud ended the conversation with the following defense of his addiction:

> *You're not a smoker. You don't understand. I was not allowed to smoke for two years. It was horrible. It felt like a good friend had died and I had to mourn him from morning to evening. Now I even have the same feelings for my pipe. She is a good friend of mine, my counsellor, my comfort, my guide, who smooths my way.*[5]

As an orally addictive phenomenon, smoking indexes the earliest phases of infantile development that haunt adulthood. Given the later development of Freud's own oral cancer, it also suggests a specifically psychoanalytic torment: that what we desire most is very likely to destroy us.

Freud knew of the link between cancer and smoking. Writing to his main acolyte Ernest Jones in 1923, after removal of a growth on his jaw, he acknowledged: "Smoking is accused as the etiology of this tissue-rebellion."[6] Freud's utter dependence on smoking can also be seen in another comment he made, this time in a letter in 1922, written to his friend and colleague, Lou Andreas Salomé, when his beloved daughter Anna was away. He had long been sorry for Anna, he said, "for still being at home with us old folks." However, "if she really were to go away, I should feel myself as deprived as I do now, and as I should do if I had to give up smoking!"[7]

This material on smoking makes the early meetings of the Wednesday Society seem like séances, with their sense of something supernatural going on, obscured by smoke. And indeed, this was not far from the truth. The occult was a regular topic of study and discussion among the psychoanalysts. Indeed, psychoanalysis itself was a kind of occult phenomenon, dealing with recesses of the mind and strange experiences that most people were not keen to touch, or thought of as somehow unhealthy. Even though Freud was in most respects a hard-headed materialist who understood the limits of hypnosis and suggestion and did not believe in ghosts, he was also a believer in telepathy and was highly superstitious. For instance, he thought he would die at various ages, as Peter Gay describes:

> For years he harboured the haunting belief that he was destined to die at the age of fifty-one, and later, at sixty-one or sixty-two; he felt pursued by these fateful ciphers as reminders of his own mortality. Even the telephone number he was assigned in 1899–14362—became confirmation: he had published *The Interpretation of Dreams* at forty-three, and the last two digits, he was convinced, were an ominous monition that sixty-two was indeed to be his life's span. Freud once analyzed superstition as a cover for hostile, murderous wishes, and his own superstitions as a suppressed desire for immortality. But his self-analysis did not completely free Freud from this bit of irrationality.[8]

The early analysts were like occultists, dealing in their rowdy way with inexplicable unconscious material just surfacing, like ghosts appearing from another world and intruding into a somewhat sordid (because smoke-filled) set of everyday surroundings. They were also creating a kind of secret society in which passionate encounters were the norm, and around which the necessary precautions that later psychoanalysts used to protect themselves had not yet been imposed, or even thought about. For instance, psychoanalysts nowadays do not treat their family members or close friends, and although there are still difficulties created by the way trainee analysts are analyzed by people who might also be participating as teachers in their training—or will almost certainly see them at Society meetings—this confusion of roles is mostly handled with great care. In the early days, however, the Wednesday Society was more like a fractious family than a professional organization. Roudinesco notes that when the early analysts presented case material they were often talking about themselves or those close to them:

> In a word, they formed a sort of extended family and they resembled their patients, who were from the same social class. A number of them were in treatment with Freud for their pathologies, and several began to treat their own family members, or else sent them to see Freud or one of their colleagues. Spouses, lovers and sisters thus became patients and, later, therapists. As for the children of the members of this first circle, they were the first to experience the Freudian treatment, which some of the disciples began to practice in 1904.[9]

This unboundedness lasted for some time. Freud treated his daughter Anna and wrote about her in one of his more famous articles, published in 1919 as "A Child is Being Beaten"[10]; Carl Jung presented his own daughter as a case during his American lectures in 1911[11]; the later analyst Melanie Klein also treated her children, and at one point she had the British psychoanalyst Ernest Jones' wife and children in analysis at the same time.[12] This lack of boundaries and openness of the unconscious of each member of Freud's circle to his and others' perusal no doubt fueled the flames of rivalry, also creating a sense of intimacy and radical innovation. The group was clearly on a voyage of discovery, and a very rocky one.

Among those who deviated from Freudian principles was psychiatrist Alfred Adler, who from the start was an unconvinced recruit to the cause of sexuality, preferring to see biological weakness as the source of a symptomatic "protest" in neurotic individuals. While Adler's theoretical divergence was tolerated for many years, as the Society gradually developed and formalized itself into a genuinely psychoanalytic grouping, with rules, principles, and a more explicit mission, it became more difficult for him to maintain a place among the Freudians. Interestingly and somewhat surprisingly, Adler nevertheless managed to remain within the fold for some time, developing his notions of "masculine protest" and focusing on aggression rather than sexuality as the core concern of what eventually came to be called Adlerian "Individual Psychology." It was not until 1911 that he stepped down from his position as Chair of the Vienna Society (Stekel left the Society at the same time). Even after his departure, Adler continued to attend the Society meetings for a while, until he was removed from his position on one of the Society's major journals, the *Zentralblatt*, at which point he finally left, taking several other analysts with him.

The process of formalizing the Vienna Society had moved forward significantly after several prominent foreigners visited it and had been unimpressed by the chaotic state of affairs there. In some cases, they were also dismayed by the almost wholly Jewish fraternity that constituted the Wednesday group. Carl Jung was one of those visitors, and an unhealthy dose of antisemitism certainly informed his response, even if Freud agreed with his Swiss colleague and others about the sad intellectual level of his followers. In any event, by 1908 the Wednesday society had become the Vienna Psychoanalytic Society, and soon afterward the first international gathering of analysts took place in Salzburg, marking the start of a genuinely international movement. Jung announced this gathering in a flyer sent to all interested analysts: "From many quarters the followers of Freud's teachings have expressed a desire for an annual meeting which would afford them an opportunity to discuss their practical experiences and to exchange ideas. Since Freud's followers, though few in numbers at present, are scattered all over Europe, it had been suggested that our first meeting should take place immediately after this year's 3rd Congress for Experimental Psychology in Frankfurt (22–25 April), so as to facilitate the attendance of colleagues from Western Europe."[13]

As Makari points out, most of the forty people who actually turned up were from Vienna or Zurich, though twenty-three came from elsewhere, including Budapest, Berlin, London (Ernest Jones) and New York (Abraham Brill). But while attendance was low, the influence of those who met in 1908 was substantial in terms of going back to establish or advance psychoanalysis in their home countries. At this conference, Freud delivered his paper on the "Rat Man," an obsessional patient with sadistic sexual fantasies.[14] Apparently, he spoke for five hours on this topic to an audience desperate for information on how to conduct a properly Freudian psychoanalysis. Following this Congress, the international movement steadily grew, as did Freud's reputation as an extraordinary innovator and creative genius. Ironically, some work had always to be done to ensure Freud's dominance among his fellows, sometimes literally. At the 1911 Weimar Congress, for instance, Freud stood on a concealed stepladder for the official picture with his disciples, to conceal his short stature and make him a giant among his peers.

Growth of a Movement

Throughout this period of growth and gradual establishment of the psychoanalytic movement, Freud sustained strong relationships with men who would become very famous themselves as founders of, and contributors to, the psychoanalytic movement. These included Sándor Ferenczi, Otto Rank, A. A. Brill and, perhaps most importantly in terms of institution building, the Welshman Ernest Jones. Jones had many complexities and was initially not much liked by Freud, but he sustained a loyal and devoted relationship with him, becoming his official biographer in the 1950s. Jones can probably be given much of the credit for the international success of the movement. He famously described himself as the "Shabbos goy" to the psychoanalysts, which says something about his view of his own ethnic strangeness as well as revealing a sympathetic and warm sense of how the specific formation of the psychoanalytic movement—notably, its rootedness in Jewish thought and culture—was crucial to its nature.[15] It also expressed the idea that the Jewish analysts needed a non-Jew to make psychoanalysis scientifically and medically acceptable, which, because of their identity (albeit not their religious beliefs), they found hard to do. Jones was better at organization than his squabbling comrades, and the usefulness to the movement of this sympathetic non-Jew in a position of institutional power was immense during the dark Nazi period. It seems as though Jones' links with Freud and the Jewish Viennese gave him a sense of his own exoticism, as well as a setting in which his capacity for imaginative service could shine and be appreciated.

Among all these relationships, assiduously maintained by Freud in meetings and through an extraordinary output of letters, one stands out as a personal struggle and tragedy, and the stuff of legend. This was his relationship with his sometime "crown prince" and the "Joshua" to his "Moses"—as he called him in two letters in 1909—the Swiss psychiatrist Carl Gustav Jung.[16] Jung's background was religious and fraught, with a depressed father, over-attentive mother, and a wider family addicted to occultism and séances. Indeed, occultism was a major theme in Jung's life, and it became one of the issues that estranged him from Freud. Before his involvement with psychoanalysis, he was deeply engaged with "psychic" experiments, including séances with his young cousin Helly Preiswerk. She was the subject of his doctoral dissertation in 1902, entitled "On the Psychology and Pathology of So-Called Occult Phenomena." This dissertation interpreted supposedly supernatural phenomena as psychological in origin. In truth, Jung never renounced an attachment to the idea of the supernatural, even if it might be linked to psychological forces. Perhaps the term "psychic" is doubly appropriate for his understanding of the mind: it conjures up the idea of the "psyche" but also of the occult.

It was not, however, as an occultist but as a scientist that Jung came to Freud's attention and Freud to his. Employed at the great psychiatric hospital in Zurich, the Burghölzli, by the pioneering psychiatrist and supporter of Freud, Eugen Bleuler, Jung carried out both clinical work and experimental investigations with the "word association test" on both neurotic and psychotic patients. The word association test was an important innovation in relation to Freudian thought. Through examining the content of patients' associations to words with which they were presented and the latency (delay) in their responses, it seemed to become possible to document and measure the unconscious, and particularly the degree of repression of uncomfortable ideas. Basically, the content of associations might say something about a person's unconscious fantasies, while latency indicated where disturbing ideas were being resisted. Jung also applied the test to himself and to other staff at the hospital. He showed that even in "normal" respondents these patterns of association and repression applied, implying that everyone, not just disturbed people, had an unconscious life of the kind proposed by Freud.

This work was written up in Jung's 1906 book, *Diagnostic Association Studies*, a copy of which he sent to Freud. Freud responded with the following opening to what became an enormous correspondence, mapping the rise and decline of a passionate relationship over the next seven years:

> 11 April 1906, IX. Berggasse 19
> Dear Colleague,
> Many thanks for sending me your *Diagnostic Association Studies*, which in my impatience I had already acquired. Of course your latest paper, 'Psychoanalysis and Association Experiments', pleased me most, because in it you argue on the strength of your own experience that everything I have said about the hitherto unexplored fields of our discipline is true. I am confident that you will often be in a position to back me up, but I shall also gladly accept correction.
> Yours sincerely, Dr Freud.[17]

Quite a lot in this short letter foreshadows the two men's later relationship, specifically on Freud's part: over-eagerness, the hope that Jung would support him, and a slightly less convincing assertion that he would "gladly accept correction." On Jung's side, there was also great excitement, but from the start, there were indications that he would not necessarily always agree with his older mentor. A letter of December 29, 1906, from Jung to Freud, identifies some early "Specific corrections of your views" which "derive from the fact that we do not see eye to eye on certain points." Jung went on to explain why these differences might have occurred, in some ways minimizing them, but in others accurately identifying their rather deeply engrained sources.

> This may be because (I) my material is totally different from yours. I am working under enormously difficult conditions mostly with uneducated insane patients, and on top of that with the uncommonly tricky material of Dementia praecox. (II) my upbringing, my milieu, and my scientific premises are in any case utterly different from your own. (III) my experience compared with yours is extremely small. (IV) both in quantity and quality of

> psychoanalytic talent the balance is distinctly in your favour. (V) the lack of personal contact with you …[18]

It is hard to know how honest Jung was being in writing this, and how much was politeness and flattery. But as Makari notes, Jung's second point is very much on target, and in many ways sums up everything that was to come.

> Different upbringing. Different milieu. Different scientific premises. In that mouthful, Jung pierced to the heart of the differences between the Zurich and Viennese Freudians. One group was Jewish, the other Protestant. One group resided in sexually open Vienna, the other in buttoned-down Zurich. One had a foot in biophysics and psychophysics, and the other was committed to the new kind of lab-based study of psychology that had emerged from a rejection of those approaches.[19]

Indeed, many writers have wondered how, given the differences between the two men, their relationship lasted for the seven years that it did. Joel Whitebook, for instance, comments, "An arrangement of reciprocal self-deception made it possible for this thoroughly improbable relationship to take hold and maintain itself for an improbable stretch of time. Each man was convinced he could convert the other to his point of view. The theory of sexuality, which Freud believed provided the litmus test for his entire position, constituted the major point of contention between them."[20] This is certainly correct, with the differences being temperamental, historical, religious-cultural, and scientific.

Yet these divergences were also in part what attracted Freud to Jung and explained what otherwise might seem to be the extraordinary over-eagerness—almost like "love at first sight"—with which he welcomed Jung into the psychoanalytic fold. For example, when Jung paid his first visit to Freud in Vienna in March 1907, Freud turned up at the hotel at which Jung and his wife were staying, bearing flowers and an invitation to dinner. That dinner famously turned into an epic conversation lasting thirteen hours (according to Jung). Even at this very early stage, however, Freud clearly picked up something agitating about the Swiss psychiatrist. During the discussion, a loud cracking noise was heard from the furniture. Jung predicted another would occur, and when it did, he claimed he saw Freud, who had dismissed his prediction as superstition, wilt—an indication perhaps of the degree of psychic intensity between the men, but certainly of the difference in their attitude to the supernatural. In other ways, however, Freud was on firm territory, interpreting a dream of Jung's as indicating a wish to displace him, again a theme that would haunt their relationship throughout.

Freud versus Jung

After the Vienna meeting, on March 31, 1907, Jung wrote Freud a letter of homage, but he did not neglect to include in it an indication of where he parted from Freud. Unfortunately, this happened to be on a point of absolute principle for Freud: the centrality of sexuality to psychological disorders. Jung was doubtful, both in terms of the theory itself—for instance, he did not see sexuality as central to psychotic disorders—but also because of the resistance that the sex-centeredness of psychoanalysis was provoking in others who might otherwise be more open to the Freudian perspective. "It has however become quite clear to me," he wrote, "that the expression 'libido' and in general all the terms ... that have been carried over into the broadened conception of sexuality are open to misunderstanding, or at least are not of didactic value. They actually evoke emotional inhibitions which make any kind of teaching impossible." Moreover, he suggested that "the sexual terminology should be reserved only for the most extreme forms of your 'libido' and that a less offensive collective term should be established for all the libidinal manifestations."[21] In other words, Freudian pansexuality was a problem and should be resolved by (a) recognizing that not all libido is sexual, and (b) expressing the sexual focus of psychoanalysis more cautiously. Freud would go a long way to maintain his links with Jung, but not as far as that.

There was also what might now be called the "ethnic" or even "cultural" difference between the two men, but in some ways, it is more appropriately coded, as it was then, as "racial." Jung's Christian or "Aryan" background was very important for Freud, who was very concerned about the Jewish domination of psychoanalysis (until Jung and another Swiss psychiatrist, Ludwig Binswanger visited in 1907, all the members of the early Vienna society except Rudolf Reitler were Jewish or converted from Judaism). For Freud, this disturbed his vision for psychoanalysis as a universal science, as opposed to what he dismissively thought of as a "Jewish national affair." Indeed, this is the exact formation Freud gave in a letter to his ultra-loyal Jewish follower, Karl Abraham, in 1908 when Abraham had been complaining about Jung and hinting at his antisemitism:

> Be tolerant, and do not forget that really it is easier for you to follow my thoughts than it is for Jung, since to begin with you are completely independent, and then you are closer to my intellectual constitution through racial kinship, while he as a Christian and a pastor's son finds his way to me only against great inner resistances. His association with us is therefore all the more valuable. I was almost going to say that it was only by his emergence on the scene that psychoanalysis was removed from the danger of becoming a Jewish national affair.[22]

Freud's recognition in this letter both of his own similarity to Abraham ("racial kinship") and his difference from Jung is a very important one. Initially, it was what made Jung valuable—a non-Jewish advocate of psychoanalysis with impeccable scientific credentials. Gradually, Jung's clear antisemitic tendencies (which manifested themselves sordidly in the 1930s, when the Nazis came to power in Germany) became bound up with his intellectual resistance to Freud, fanning the flames of ill-will.

Jung was always an erratic follower of Freud, and an erratic person to boot. His treatment of his own patients in Zurich was also not always exemplary. Famously, his relationships could get out of hand, as was the case with the Russian Sabina Spielrein, who was a patient of Jung's before becoming his lover. Later, she attended Freud's group in Vienna (where she was one of the sources for his idea of the "Death Drive"). She returned to practice psychoanalysis in Russia in the 1920s, but was shot dead by the Nazis in 1942. Jung exploited her and lied about her. Freud initially covered this up before rebuking his Swiss colleague in an ambiguous way, at the same time introducing an important new idea, that of "countertransference," here meaning the unconscious baggage that an analyst might bring to the encounter with a patient, which must be dealt with if treatment is to be successful. Faced with unequivocal evidence of Jung's misdemeanors, Freud wrote (letter of June 7, 1909), "Such experiences, though painful, are necessary and hard to avoid. Without them we cannot really know life and what we are dealing with. I myself have never been taken in quite so badly, but I have come very close to it a number of times and had a *narrow escape* … But no lasting harm is done. They help us to develop the thick skin we need and to dominate 'countertransference.'" He added that they are a "*blessing in disguise*."[23] On the face of it, this "defense" excused Jung and minimized his offense, a reading made more viable by the classically misogynistic next line: "The way these women manage to charm us with every conceivable psychic perfection until they have attained their purpose is one of nature's greatest spectacles."[24] Yet there is also a rebuke in the letter—a warning to Jung not to let his own impulses overcome him, but instead to recognize that they are part of the psychoanalytical process, and have to be treated carefully and professionally as such.

Despite his instability, Jung was an enormous help to the fledgling psychoanalytic movement in the years from 1907. But there was always trouble around him. The most famous early exhibition of this came with Freud's otherwise triumphant visit to America in 1909, after an invitation by the great American psychologist G. Stanley Hall to receive an honorary degree at Clark University. Jung was also invited (after another attendee withdrew), and Freud asked Hungarian psychoanalyst Sándor Ferenczi to accompany them. The trip itself was a substantial undertaking, made worse by tensions between Freud and Jung over authority and rebellion (as ever). Just before the sea voyage began, Jung told a story about mummified bodies found in German peat bogs, which Freud interpreted as a death wish directed at him—a realization that caused Freud to faint. On the voyage itself, Freud interpreted Jung's dreams as rivalrous ones, while avoiding exposing himself, acutely disgruntling Jung. This did not seem to affect the two men's performance in America. Faced with a highly illustrious audience, Freud gave a masterfully clear account of psychoanalysis (in German), not pulling any punches about sexuality and yet apparently convincing his audience of the scientific validity and novelty of the new approach. These lectures were subsequently published as *Five Lectures on Psychoanalysis*, and remain among the clearest introductions to the subject. The editors' introduction to them in the Standard Edition of Freud's work is instructive about his excited response to his American invitation, despite Freud's cynicism about America itself (he is reputed to have said that it was "gigantic—that is, a gigantic mistake"). It also says something about his working methods.

> It was in December, 1908, that Freud first received the invitation, but it was not until the following autumn that the event took place,

> and Freud's five lectures were delivered on Monday, September 6, 1909, and the four following days. This, as Freud himself declared at the time, was the first official recognition of the young science, and he has described in his Autobiographical Study how, as he stepped on to the platform to deliver his lectures, "it seemed like the realization of some incredible day-dream." The lectures (in German, of course) were, according to Freud's almost universal practice, delivered extempore and, as we learn from Dr. Jones, without notes and after very little preparation. It was only after his return to Vienna that he was induced unwillingly to write them out. This work was not finished till the second week of December, but his verbal memory was so good that, as Dr. Jones assures us, the printed version "did not depart much from the original delivery."[25]

Jung also lectured, giving some compelling case material, and the men went home satisfied, if not necessarily completely at ease with one another.

Things then began to unravel, fueled by misunderstandings, vaunting ambition, and Freud's characteristic fluctuations between gloom and combativeness. Jung became more interested in religion, seeing psychoanalysis as part of a post-Christian spiritual revival, and moved further away from Freud's notions of the specifically sexual nature of the libido. Freud himself started to experiment with interpretations of mythology, which Jung had always been interested in, leading to the publication in 1913 of his "anthropological" work, *Totem and Taboo*. This text presented an account of the founding of society as rooted in the murder of the primal father by his sons—a provocative "just-so" story that had a lot of resonance for those on both sides of the Freud-Jung debate. In 1912, an attempt was made to patch things up, but the relationship only got worse. During a discussion of the Egyptian Pharaoh Akhenaten, who had overthrown his father's religion (itself a remarkable commentary on what was exercising psychoanalytic minds then), Freud fainted again and had to be picked up by Jung and carried to another room. Shortly after this, relations between the two men came to an end.

The final letters testify both to the rancor and to the explicitness with which these great psychologists were willing to twist the knife into each other. First, Jung, who on December 11–14, 1912, made a slip, writing "Even Adler's cronies do not regard me as one of yours," when he meant "one of theirs."[26] Freud seized on this in his reply: "Are you 'objective' enough to consider the following slip without anger? Even Adler's cronies do not regard me as one of *yours*. Yours nevertheless, Freud."[27] In response, Jung wrote on December 18, 1912: "Your technique of treating your pupils like patients is a *blunder* … I am objective enough to see through your little trick. You go around sniffing out all the symptomatic actions in your vicinity, thus reducing everyone to the level of sons and daughters who blushingly admit the existence of their faults. Meanwhile you remain on top as the father, sitting pretty … You see, dear Professor, as long as you hand out this stuff I don't give a damn for my symptomatic actions; they shrink to nothing."[28] Freud's answer on January 3, 1913, was irrevocable: "It is a convention among us analysts that none of us need feel ashamed of his own bit of neurosis. But one who while behaving abnormally keeps shouting that he is normal gives ground for the suspicion that he lacks insight into his illness. Accordingly, I propose that we abandon our personal relations entirely. I shall lose nothing by it, for my only emotional tie with you has long been a thin thread—the lingering effect of past disappointments … "[29] And finally Jung, a couple of days later: "I accede to your wish that we abandon our personal relations, for I never thrust my friendship on anyone. You yourself are the best judge of what this moment means to you. 'The rest is silence.'"[30]

Perhaps surprisingly, Jung's professional relationship with the Freudian movement continued for another year. At the Nuremberg Congress of 1910, Jung had been proposed as Life President of the International Psychoanalytical Association; only a rebellion by the Viennese analysts had prevented this from happening, and he was appointed for only two years. By the time the fourth International Psychoanalytical Congress met in Munich in September 1913, battle lines were more firmly drawn, and though Jung was re-elected, it was against a significant amount of opposition. Feeling that Freud's supporters were ganging up on him—which they were—Jung resigned his editorship of one of the main psychoanalytic journals and then, in April 1914, he resigned completely from the psychoanalytic movement. Soon afterward, in the wake of Freud's tendentious little book, *On the History of the Psychoanalytic Movement*, he was followed into the wilderness by almost all the other members of the Zurich society. A year before this, in January 1913, a "secret committee" of loyalists had been formed around Freud. Its members—Ernest Jones, Sándor Ferenczi, Karl Abraham, Otto Rank, and Hans Sachs—did not all remain loyal forever. But they certainly saw out, and even partly provoked, the Jung crisis, and made Freud feel safe, wanted, and admired, secure in his hopes that the psychoanalytic movement would not collapse with the departure of its "crown prince."

Much more could be said about this fervid history, but perhaps one point is worth making before moving on. Psychoanalysis is a reflexive discipline, aware that the processes of its own adherents are themselves subject to the unconscious irrationalities, wishes, and fantasies that characterize its discovery about human life. This awareness, however, has never stopped it re-enacting exactly those same irrationalities and, at times, self-destructive impulses in the dealings of its members with one another, in their personal lives, and in their professional societies.

6

War and Its Aftermath

It should have come as no surprise to Freud that European civilization might harbor destructive elements. After all, the idea of the Freudian unconscious is that, no matter how "cultured" we may be, inner wishes and impulses are seeking to break through in what Freud referred to in *Totem and Taboo* as a "primitive" way. And while up to the time of the First World War the forces operating in the unconscious were understood to be mainly sexual and therefore life-enhancing, they were also seen as potentially socially disruptive, which is why at times they would need to be "repressed." Freud was never particularly confident that the unconscious could be managed and he was certainly no great optimist when it came either to human nature or to the benevolence of society. As noted previously, at the end of the early text *Studies on Hysteria*, Freud had commented about the limited aims and prospects of psychoanalysis as a cure.[1] Although Freud's attitude toward the treatment aims of psychoanalysis varied from time to time, he was never a therapeutic enthusiast, and rarely wavered from the idea that people are not really made for happiness. Pleasure is fleeting, he thought, and suffering is always the more likely reality.

Oddly, when war came in 1914, Freud was swept up for a while in the patriotic enthusiasm of the time, sharing his countrymen's belief that the war would be swift and that the Central Powers—Austria-Hungary, Germany, Bulgaria and the Ottoman Empire—would triumph. This state of mind did not last very long. It was replaced by a dismal awareness of the overwhelming destructiveness of the war, along with realistic concerns for his three sons and his son-in-law, who had all enlisted, plus the increasingly dire and isolated situation of the psychoanalytic movement. Fortunately, although one of Freud's nephews was killed in the war, his family escaped relatively unscathed, with his sons Martin, Oliver, and Ernst, as well as Freud's daughter Sophie's husband Max Halberstadt, all returning safely. Nevertheless, there was widespread hardship and long-term consequences that would change Freud, his theory, and the psychoanalytic movement.

Freud's psychoanalytic practice nearly dried up during the war. By the end of 1914, he had only one remaining patient, and it was difficult for him to maintain contact with his followers and friends spread around Europe. He managed to travel occasionally, memorably visiting his daughter Sophie in Hamburg in 1915. During that trip, he made some observations about his infant grandson Ernst that prompted Freud to rework his psychoanalytic drive theory at the end of the decade. But mostly he was stuck in Vienna, increasingly short of money and despondent about the future of the psychoanalytic movement and of the world in general. Characteristically, however, Freud's extraordinary capacity for creative work came to the fore, and the absence of external distractions such as patients and meetings gave him the time to embark on a set of new writings that showed him still able to reconsider the basics of his science, and to reinvent it for a post-cataclysmic society.

During the war, Freud's writings were to some extent backward-looking and integrating, in the sense that they pulled together material that he had worked on for some time and tried to give them an overarching shape that would make them into a single system. Freud's general approach was "accretionary": he would often add new ideas to old ones, frequently by inserting footnotes into previously published texts. For example, there were major changes to the *Three Essays on the Theory of Sexuality* in its various editions, announced in footnotes. This increased the liveliness of the texts and made Freud's presence as a writer even more strongly felt. At the same time, the material became more confusing. Now, during the period of reflection that the war years brought, Freud drew together some of this thinking in a series of five great "metapsychological" works—the "meta" being shorthand for "that which stands above," and hence representing a theoretical integration. These papers—the reduced output from an originally proposed set of twelve—were on the theory of the instincts; repression; the unconscious; dreams; and, least "metapsychologically" and most importantly of all, the great and nowadays widely referenced paper on grief, *Mourning and Melancholia*. Together, these papers presented a powerful, albeit difficult, integration of the Freudian framework, making it possible to see how the various components of the theory might fit together. Repression and the unconscious are indissoluble: the one presupposes the other. Instincts drive the system and operate on the boundary of biology and psychology; sometimes, they can be understood as biological "forces" and at others as representations of these forces in the mind. Dreams remain the royal road to the unconscious, as they always had been for Freud. But there were some signs of an emerging set of problems that were going to feed into a major reformulation of Freudian theory that happened at the end of the war.

While the metapsychological papers are integrative, they are not that easy to follow, and their conciseness and density meant they would become resources for psychoanalytic theorists more than for clinicians or for the general reading public. This was not true of Freud's other great synthesizing work of the war years, the *Introductory Lectures on Psychoanalysis*.[2] These were genuine lectures, unlike the later *New Introductory Lectures*, which were never given as spoken pieces. By the time the *New Introductory Lectures* were prepared, in the early 1930s, Freud's oral cancer prevented him from speaking clearly. But in the winters of 1915 and 1916, he gave a series of twenty-eight lectures "in a lecture room of the Vienna Psychiatric Clinic before an audience gathered from all the Faculties of the University," as he reported later.[3] A hundred or more students, doctors, followers, and curious outsiders attended, hearing Freud speak calmly and informally, in a phenomenally well-ordered and carefully paced way, with examples and humor. He led his audience through the fundamental premises of psychoanalysis, as derived from *The Psychopathology of Everyday Life*, *The Interpretation of Dreams*, and the *Three Essays on the Theory of Sexuality*. Freud was in his element here as a teacher. In the Preface to the *New Introductory Lectures*, written fifteen years later, he related that in the first season "the lectures were improvised, and written out immediately afterwards; drafts of the second half were made during the intervening summer vacation at Salzburg, and delivered word for word in the following winter. At that time I still possessed the gift of a photographic memory."[4]

The lectures remain a treat to read, perhaps still the best available exposition of "early" Freud, and a masterpiece of propaganda as well as of pedagogy. Carefully, patiently, amusingly, and irrefutably, Freud started from the entertaining muddles of everyday life ("parapraxes") and moved through dreams and neuroses before getting to sexuality and the final elements of therapeutic work, including the dynamite notion of transference. By this time, Freud may have been deeply depressed by the war: in Roudinesco's words, "He was irritable he committed one solecism after another; he told Jewish jokes to stave off anguish."[5] Nevertheless, there was little sign of distress in these lectures; in fact, as he turned sixty, he was at the height of his explanatory powers.

Alongside this work, something else was occupying Freud's mind. In 1914, he published a short paper, *On Narcissism: An Introduction*, which took potshots at some of his critics, notably Adler, but also identified a problem with his existing theory of the drives and of sexuality.[6] The key ideas here, within another dense but evocative text, are that narcissism is a normal part of development, and that it is characterized by the ego (the "I") taking itself as an object of sexual longing. These ideas were consistent with clinical and developmental observations, and neatly integrated some of Adler's better notions into the Freudian scheme. However, they created a problem that Freud would only be able to deal with later, when he undertook a radical revision of drive theory. The problem was that Freud envisaged the drives as conflicting forces, out of which diverging psychological events were generated. For example, neurotic symptoms were seen as a kind of compromise between unconscious wishes and the behaviors that are acceptable to consciousness. The forces that Freud recognized at this time were sexuality and those that he called "ego-preservative," which basically served other needs (such as hunger) and protected the ego against the untrammeled demands of sexuality. What narcissism suggested, however, was a breakdown in this clear division. The crucial point was that Freud was forced to recognize that the ego contains sexual instincts, which might themselves be providing the source of energy for what had hitherto been seen as the separate ego-preservative instincts. Put differently, the ego could no longer be viewed as an agency separate from sex, for it was itself full of it. Freud's whole dualistic structure, which he had defended against Jung's heretical widening of the notion of libido from a specifically sexual force to the all-encompassing motor of life, was at risk. Psychoanalysis might truly reduce to pan-sexualism, just as its critics claimed.

The problematics of narcissism and the place of sexuality in the Freudian scheme continued, and perhaps fueled another great work of the period, the case study of the "Wolf Man." The patient was a Russian aristocrat called Sergei Pankejeff who famously had a dream of wolves sitting in a tree, from which his nickname derived. Freud interpreted the dream as evidence of Pankejeff having seen, and been traumatized by, sex between his parents, and he used this explanation to unpick the patient's neurosis. Unfortunately, because of some aggravating circumstances—Pankejeff losing his fortune in the Russian Revolution and Freud's over-optimistic assessment of his treatment's success—the results of the analysis were less impressive than might have been hoped. Indeed, Pankejeff became financially and psychologically dependent on psychoanalysis and psychoanalysts for the rest of his life. But it is a great story, and provides a fine narrative of infantile sexuality, contributing to Freud's literary credentials, if not so much to his scientific advances.

Mourning and Melancholia, War and Death

All this, however, can in retrospect be seen as less important than another major shift in Freud's thinking. The war was taking its toll, and Freud was faced with incontrovertible evidence of the destructive side of humanity and unavoidable exposure to the reality of suffering and loss. It is here that Freud's greatness came to the fore. However irascible he was becoming—and he had always had that tendency, but it was now aggravated by both psychological and physical pain—his mind was clearly alert to what was going on, his emotions were receptive and his feelings open, and his capacity for creative work was undiminished. In *Mourning and Melancholia*, Freud began to face up to the profundity of the issues of loss and grief, making distinctions between "healthy" mourning and chronic depression in ways that have retained their freshness and significance to this day.[7] In the process, he offered a vocabulary that could encompass both the losses that we know about and gradually come to terms with, and those that we reject and that consequently haunt us forever. In this wonderful text, Freud notes that loss is a central component of both "normal" mourning and the excessive variety that goes by the name "melancholia." It is especially the loss of a *person* that affects us, though at times it can also be what Freud calls "some abstraction which has taken the place of [a person], such as one's country, liberty, an ideal, and so on."[8] Mourning is a normal response to such losses and is characterized by sadness that gradually lifts as mourners find sources of value in the world that enable them to move on with their lives—for example, new people to love or the satisfaction embedded in new projects and activities.

Melancholia, however, is the state we might fall into when the normal process of mourning is blocked. It is a kind of interminable mourning that can never be resolved. This is often because the reality or significance of the original loss is for some reason denied. If people cannot accept that they have lost someone or something of value—perhaps because it is too distressing to consciously admit this, or too shameful—then the loss itself becomes repressed and they are left with a feeling of there being something missing that cannot be grieved for, or of emptiness, or perhaps of self-blame. This is a recipe for melancholia, or for what is now more commonly termed severe depression.

Freud describes melancholia as a response to loss that has all the attributes of mourning but is distinguished by "a profoundly painful dejection, cessation of interest in the outside world, loss of the capacity to love, inhibition of all activity, and a lowering of the self-regarding feelings to a degree that finds utterance in self-reproaches and self-revilings, and culminates in a delusional expectation of punishment."[9] This is as good a description of depression as most, but what is especially interesting about it is how it suggests that the "problem" of melancholia is of not being able to come to terms with loss because it is not properly recognized. This might be for personal reasons, having to do with the circumstances of a person's development. But in a context in which loss is unbearable, for example during the kind of vicious war that was ravaging Europe at the time *Mourning and Melancholia* was written, the full horror of what has been lost might be especially hard to come to terms with. Not surprisingly, psychic withdrawal into melancholic self-hatred that feeds on itself and is unresponsive to attempts by other people to reach out to the sufferer, will be increasingly common. It is possible to argue here that *Mourning and Melancholia* is not just a great "psychiatric" text but also a social commentary and a harbinger of the more depressive and pessimistic tone of much of Freud's writing in the latter period of his life.

Fueled by the imaginative genius of Freud's close Hungarian colleague and friend Sándor Ferenczi and the wealth of his compatriot Anton von Freund, it looked for a while as though psychoanalysis would emerge from the war stronger than before. It had proven itself useful in the treatment of war neuroses, with German psychoanalyst Ernst Simmel having presented powerful evidence of this at the Budapest Congress of the International Psychoanalytical Association in September 1918, which von Freund had bankrolled. It also seemed as if the authorities were willing to put resources into psychoanalysis to build on this success. However, the collapse of the Central Powers at the end of the war meant that the psychoanalytic movement lost its funds and had to be rebuilt. It also meant that the suffering caused by the war transitioned into the desperate privations afflicting the citizens of central Europe for years to come. In this context, it is interesting to note how life-enhancing some of Freud's thinking remained. For example, at the 1918 Congress, he made a case for free psychoanalytic treatment to be available to ordinary people, and this spawned a Free Clinic movement that bore fruit first in Berlin in 1920, and later in Budapest, Vienna, and London. The social reformism of this measure reflected a genuinely social democratic strand in Freud's thinking and in that of many members of the psychoanalytic movement. Later, the rise of Nazism destroyed this progressive approach, but at the time, Freudianism was regarded as one of the potentially great modernizing and liberating forces of the early twentieth century.

That said, the deathly side of the world had a big impact on Freud, remaining with him for the rest of his life. In 1919, he published an essay on "The Uncanny" that reflected the growing social interest in the occult and in disturbing, "ghostly" phenomena that resulted from the huge suffering and loss of the war. By 1920 and the publication of his book *Beyond the Pleasure Principle*, a new concept had entered the Freudian vocabulary: the Death Drive. This was really a remarkable turnaround for Freud. Among other things, it picked up Adler's idea about the importance of aggression, pushed sexuality aside from its dominant position in the psychoanalytic pantheon, and dealt with the trauma of the war by sidestepping trauma itself, replacing it with a notion that in each of us there is a biological drive toward self-annihilation. The logic of Freudian theory and the impact of the war both fed into these changes. The former was a response to the problems produced by narcissism, so that the opposed drives were no longer sex versus ego-preservation, but Life (including sex) against Death. The existence of the latter seemed obvious: how could the extraordinary scale of devastation left by the war be due just to a sadistic element of sexuality? And what about traumatic war neuroses and dreams? The repetitive dreams of sufferers who could not get over their experiences seemed to have little to do with the wish-fulfillments that Freud had postulated in 1900 as being at the source of all dreams.

Freud's argument for the Death Drive in *Beyond the Pleasure Principle* was consistent with his longstanding idea that satisfaction of a drive depends on reduction in tension. His model remained sexual: increase in tension due to stimulation raises excitation, but the actual fulfillment of the pleasure principle occurs when that tension dissipates and the organism—the human body and mind—returns to rest. This notion was coupled with Freud's equally longstanding commitment to the duality of drives. He wrote, "Our views have from the very first been dualistic, and to-day they are even more definitely dualistic than before—now that we describe the opposition as being, not between ego instincts and sexual instincts but between life instincts and death instincts."[10] Yet there is a paradox here, which lies in the "beyond" of

Beyond the Pleasure Principle. If all drives aim to reduce the organism to rest, which is supposed to be the essence of pleasure, then there is no drive that is "beyond." But Freud astutely recognized that while in theory this might be the case, the phenomenology of life is such that there is a complication around the nature of pleasure. For Freud, the "conservatism" of the drives programs the organism toward *return* in the sense of seeking an earlier state of affairs. Rest is something that comes when we get back to the situation before there was any disruption—any need to do anything at all. This is what makes it "beyond" pleasure: pleasure comes from the reduction in tension, but what is beyond that is the static position of complete rest. This is true for the individual but also for the species. As he writes in *Beyond the Pleasure Principle:*

> It would be in contradiction to the conservative nature of the instincts if the goal of life were a state of things which had never yet been attained. On the contrary, it must be an old state of things, an initial state from which the living entity has at one time or other departed and to which it is striving to return by the circuitous paths along which its development leads. If we are to take it as a truth that knows no exception that everything living dies for internal reasons—becomes inorganic once again—then we shall be compelled to say that "*the aim of all life is death*" and, looking backwards, that "*inanimate things existed before living ones*."[11]

We are forced to participate in life by "the history of the earth we live in and of its relation to the sun,"[12] and the drives accept this as they must, building the adaptations required into their own program. But this is not an enthusiastic embracing of life; rather, it is a way of seeking out the "circuitous paths" that will enable the organism—the human one included—to find its own way to death.

This rather dismal scenario laid the grounds for a vivid portrayal of how humankind's propensity for destructiveness—so observable then as now—is constantly in tension with its desire for life, for building comforting and generative connections with other people and the world around. Freud was always sensitive to this opposition and never quite gave up on Eros, but in the latter part of his life, it was the dark side of things that came more easily to him. There were biographical as well as intellectual and characterological sources for this. As well as the historical circumstance of the massive destruction of the First World War and the appalling demonstration that people might not be committed to preserving civilization, there was also the small moment of what is known as the "fort-da game." This was a simple game that Freud watched his grandson Ernst play and that has become the most famous game in the history of psychoanalysis. It took place in September 1915, when Ernst was just eighteen months old, while Freud was visiting his daughter Sophie in her home in Hamburg. The child was observed throwing a wooden reel into his curtained cot so that it could not be seen, and then pulling it back out again, accompanying these actions with sounds ("ooh-aah") interpreted as the German words "fort" ("gone") and "a joyful da" ("there"). Having been puzzled by the child's repeated act of throwing away his toys, Freud speculated that the game needed its two parts, and suggested that "It was related to the child's great cultural achievement—the instinctual renunciation (that is, the renunciation of instinctual satisfaction) which he had made in allowing his mother to go away without protesting. He compensated himself for this, as it were, by himself staging the disappearance and return of the objects within his reach."[13]

Freud suggested some interpretations of the game. First, it changed a passive situation into an active one, so that the boy was mastering his distress at his mother's disappearance by controlling her symbolic reappearance. Second, he might be taking pleasurable revenge on her: "In that case it would have a defiant meaning: 'All right, then, go away! I don't need you. I'm sending you away myself.'" Freud commented, "We know of other children who liked to express similar hostile impulses by throwing away objects instead of persons."[14] This is roughly where he left it: that while it might seem odd that a child should engage in the repetition of something unpleasant (symbolically re-enacting his mother's disappearance), in fact, it serves functions which in at least some respects are pleasurable, helping him master the anxiety-producing situation by making him feel less helpless, or enabling him to take symbolic revenge. But when Freud reflected on them from the point of view of the emerging idea of the Death Drive, he became interested in the repetitive way in which something unpleasant (the mother's disappearance) kept returning, having to be dealt with anew by the child each time. What can we make of this "compulsion to repeat," if it is not a sign that there is always something destructive and annihilatory pressing for return, having to be taken into account and kept at bay?

We have to be sympathetic to little Ernst. To be a talisman of repetition like this, as well as the object of gaze of one of the most influential observers in history, might be a big enough burden for a small boy. What was harder still was the continuation of the story, the bit that is not in *Beyond the Pleasure Principle* except as a passing footnote. By the time this work appeared in 1920, Sophie, Freud's "Sunday child," was dead of the Spanish flu, along with at least 20 million other people. Sophie's death destroyed her family. It was so sudden—she was ill for just five days—and so cruel; twenty-six years old and pregnant with her third child. Freud was devastated. "The undisguised brutality of our time weighs heavily on us," he wrote in a letter to his friend, the Swiss pastor Oskar Pfister;[15] and to Sándor Ferenczi, "Wafted away! Nothing to say."[16] From Peter Gay's biography, it is clear that Freud tried to manage his grief in a way consistent with his own general stoicism; as he wrote to Sophie's husband, "One must bow one's head under the blow, as a helpless, poor human being with whom higher powers are playing."[17] But clearly, his feelings were deeply stirred and never fully settled thereafter. Gay quotes Freud's encounter with a famous patient, the imagist poet H. D. (Hilda Doolittle) over a decade later, in 1933. According to H. D., whilst she and Freud were discussing the epidemic at the end of the War, Freud said "he had reason to remember the epidemic, as he lost his favourite daughter. 'She is here,' he said, and he showed me a tiny locket that he wore, fastened to his watch-chain."[18]

The situation then became even worse. Freud's childless daughter Mathilde had taken on the care of Sophie's younger son, Heinerle; his other childless, unmarried daughter Anna had taken on Ernst. There was no doubt in anyone's mind which was the more charming of the two children: Heinerle was an exceptionally "taking" little boy. But in 1923, aged only four, he died of tuberculosis, an event that devastated his grandfather, who possibly loved this child more than he had ever loved anyone before. Freud was deeply absorbed in his own distress. "I find this loss very hard to bear, I don't think I have ever experienced such grief," he wrote at the time, in a letter to Katja Levy, Anton von Freund's sister.[19] Ernest Jones stated that it was the only occasion on which Freud was known to shed tears, and that he said the boy's death had "killed something in him for good." Three years later, writing to Swiss psychiatrist Ludwig Binswanger, whose own young child had just died, Freud commented, "For me, that child took the place of all my children and other grandchildren, and since then, since Heinerle's death, I have no longer cared for my grandchildren, but find no enjoyment in life either."[20] In the aftermath of Heinerle's death, Freud also wrote that his other grandson Ernst provided no consolation, and it was fortunate that Anna took Ernst on as his substitute mother and analyst, or the little boy might have been utterly neglected. As it was, he had many problems, despite being the only one of Freud's grandchildren who became a psychoanalyst.[21]

The Ego and the Id

The other major biographical contribution to the focus on death was Freud's own declining health, and especially his cancer. As previously described, Freud was an intense and inveterate smoker, and for years he deceived himself into thinking that this habit was not harmful, even though he knew it was. By 1923, he had to have his first operation. Because of his ambivalence and the failure of his personal doctor, Felix Deutsch, who was also one of his followers, to face up to the truth of the severity of Freud's illness, the operation was entrusted to a less than competent surgeon, who botched it. Freud then called in a first-rate doctor, Hans Pichler, who carried out the first of over two dozen surgeries on his patient. These operations left Freud with huge cavities in his mouth and jaw, as well as dependence on a prosthesis that impeded his eating and speaking. Roudinesco summarizes a long period of suffering and in many respects heroic stoicism on Freud's part and, it should be added, on the part of his daughter-nurse Anna:

> Freud had to undergo several types of operations: some under local anesthetics and sedation, others under general anesthesia. After each one, he had difficulty speaking, and over the years it became harder and harder for him to eat; he also suffered from deafness in his right ear, so he was obliged to adjust the placement of his couch in order to hear his patients correctly. The prosthesis had to be cleaned, readjusted, and repositioned, at the price of endless pain. When Freud was unable to put it back in place, he called for Anna's help; she sometimes struggled with the "monster" for an hour.[22]

At the time of writing, the prosthesis is on display at the Freud Museum London, an example of the fetishization of all things Freudian that has persisted for the best part of a century.

From the early 1920s onward, Anna became Freud's representative, delivering his papers at Congresses and presenting his views to the outside world. He became increasingly dependent on her and relieved that she never left him, despite concerns about her lack of an erotic life that prompted him to take her into analysis from 1918 to 1924. As noted earlier, this crossing of boundaries was not as unusual then as it would be now. But even in the 1920s, it would have raised eyebrows if people had generally known about it, as they might have done with the publication in 1920 of Freud's thinly disguised account of his daughter's fantasies, *A Child is Being Beaten*. A bit later, Anna also published her own version, called *The Relation of Beating-Phantasies to a Day-Dream*, using it as her reading-in paper to the Vienna Psychoanalytic Society in 1922, when she "officially" became a psychoanalyst.[23] There is some suggestion that Freud realized at this time that Anna's erotic life was directed more toward women than men. Nevertheless, while she later formed a lifelong liaison with the American heiress and child psychoanalyst Dorothy Burlingham, her first and strongest attachment was always to her father.

A final strand in Freud's work in this period reflected his integrative tendencies, but in a way which yet again revolutionized the Freudian field. This was his book of 1923, *The Ego and the Id*, which introduced a new "structural" model of the mind, the very famous division between ego, id, and superego. This idea of "structure" suggests something fixed and perhaps at odds with the "dynamic" nature of Freud's vision of the unconscious as something always pressing for expression, causing disruption and trouble as it goes. However, it is worth noting the difference between the associations of Freud's German-language terminology and the effects of the work of his English translators from the 1920s until the 1950s. To describe the conscious self, Freud referred to "das Ich," the "I." What he was evoking was the sense each one of us has of being a center of consciousness, from which our thoughts and feelings proceed. The decision of the translators to render this homely notion as "the ego" deliberately distanced psychoanalysis from this everyday mode, making it more seemingly "scientific," but also more alien. The ego became a formal system rather than an experience. Similarly, "das Es," translated (into Latin!) as the "id," actually means the "it." This conveys very well the experience of having something within ourselves that feels alien and threatens to dominate us, and this seems to have been exactly Freud's intention. The id is full of primeval and repressed unconscious impulses, which are both part of "us," and yet somehow not owned; we are constituted in large part by something over which we have limited knowledge and control. The third structural agency is similarly alienated in the translation. The "superego" is, in fact, the "Over-I" ("das Über-Ich"), an internal entity that watches over us, judging and condemning us and originating feelings of guilt.

In his earlier writing, Freud mainly used the term "the ego" to refer to the conscious self. His notion was that the ego was an active part of the mind, present from the beginning of life in some form and containing the energy of the ego-preservative drives. Even after the development of his theory of narcissism, he still thought of the ego as the main source of psychic energy: "the ego is the true and original reservoir of libido, and … it is only from that reservoir that libido is extended onto objects," he wrote in *Beyond the Pleasure Principle*.[24] But in *The Ego and the Id*, Freud revised his views. Interestingly, his source for his new way of formulating things was at least as much philosophical and literary as it was "scientific." Perhaps he was searching for a way to express the insight that we are often "lived" by forces beyond us.

> Now I think we shall gain a great deal by following the suggestion of a writer who, from personal motives, vainly asserts that he has nothing to do with the rigours of pure science. I am speaking of Georg Groddeck, who is never tired of insisting that what we call our ego behaves essentially passively in life, and that, as he expresses it, we are "lived" by unknown and uncontrollable forces.[25]

This is the introduction to the "id" or "it" as the home of the repressed and of fundamental drives. It is the source of energy, out of which unconscious drive impulses flow. It compels us to act in ways we do not necessarily choose, and its contents are unconscious, so hidden away. It is, therefore, the incarnation of alienation, something we are each haunted by: an "other" within us. But although everything in the id is unconscious, not all that is unconscious is in the id: consciousness and structure do not go together. Both the ego and the second new invention in *The Ego and the Id*, the superego, can hold unconscious material inside them.

With the creation of the id, Freud's notion of the ego changed quite dramatically. The ego was now seen as arising out of the id, developing from perception and consciousness, but also by "taking in" experiences of objects. Among other things, this means that, faced with the unavoidable losses that all humans experience (for example, separation from the mother), the ego internalizes a representation of the lost object and makes it part of itself. The ego thus comes to be a home for lost desires and forsaken objects, which are absorbed along with the id-originated psychic energy invested in them. This, Freud writes, "makes it possible to suppose that the character of the ego is a precipitate of abandoned object-cathexes and that it contains the history of those object choices."[26] The ego is developed largely through identification with things it values and loves in the outside world ("cathexes" can be understood as "emotional investments"), which become the template for the structural development of the personality. The theory also links the structural model with the darker side of Freud's thought: development of the "I" is in large part a process of mourning those we have lost.

As can perhaps be seen, Freud's model of ego-id-superego is a useful one in that it allows us to picture what a mind might have to do to cope with the complexities of unconscious ideas as they make themselves felt. Unconscious ideas pump away, demanding things, and the ego has to mediate between them and reality, so that the individual does not suffer too much. They are amoral and potentially dissolute, and it is the task of the superego to maintain standards, even if by doing so the individual becomes overly constrained. This explains why people so often feel at odds with themselves, and why it is so common to see good people wracked by guilt. They are "good" because of the severity of their superego, which in turn explains why all their goodness does not stop them from feeling bad. The structural model also offers a language in which we might describe some very complicated issues, such as how mourning takes place, why some people seem to have no conscience at all, and how it can be that in our essence, we might feel that we are "other" to ourselves.

7

Late Freud

When Hitler came to power in Germany in 1933, Freud was seventy-six years old, suffering from advanced cancer of the jaw, and tetchy and poor. He was supported by wealthy foreign patients paying him high fees in cash (25 dollars an hour, perhaps equivalent to around $500 today). He relied for care on his daughter Anna (his "Antigone").[1] He was also wrestling with his Jewish identity, as evidenced in the devotion of much of his last few years of life to completing his book on Judaism, *Moses and Monotheism*.[2] In the literary and political critic Edward Said's influential reading, he was embarking on his "late style," characterized not by relaxation into contented old age or the drawing together of an integrated version of a life's work, but rather to "intransigence and a sort of irascible transgressiveness, as if the author was expected to settle down into harmonious composure, as befits a person at the end of his life, but preferred instead to be difficult, and to bristle with all sorts of new ideas and provocations."[3] Said's main example of this is *Moses and Monotheism* itself, which not only—as Freud himself recognized—challenges Jewish self-esteem in supposing that Moses was an Egyptian, but also demonstrates a willingness to rethink some of Freud's own previous ideas on social identity. That is, in the appalling years after the Nazis came to power, Freud was engaged in finding ways to stay physically and mentally alive.

Faced with oppression, exile and death, Freud's bad-tempered refusal to go quietly is perhaps the keenest way in which Freud's "resistance" during this period can be conceptualized. We need to stay aware here of the poignant nuances of the psychoanalytic notion of resistance as the avoidance of psychic truth and of its contrast with the *political* idea of resistance—and of how both apply to Freud's condition throughout his life, and never more so than in the 1930s. The key resonance of political resistance is as a force opposed to a greater force, a liberatory activity set against an oppressive structure. As power assaults it, resistance stands firm. In this sense, resistance is what the *healthy* subject does, refusing to be cowed. Of course, the imagery must be more complex here: governments resist the will of the people, and so on; but it seems fair to argue that the main association of political resistance is that it comes *from* the people against those who would take away their liberties. In the context of Europe under the shadow of Nazism, resistance was infused into all the small and great acts of those who tried to stand up against oppression and refuse to be dominated by it, usually, as we know, at enormous personal risk. Freud was too old and weak to do much, but he was certainly not cowed, however frightened he might have been at times.

Leaving Austria

As a title of the final chapter of his biography *Freud: A Life for our Time*, Peter Gay took Freud's famous comment in a letter to his son Ernst, then in London, in March 1938: "Two prospects survive in these trying times, to see you all together and to die in freedom."[4] To die in freedom: even such a small comment is an act of resistance toward a vicious ruling party seeking to seize on any sign of dissent and to wipe it out. Freud's response to Anna when she was unsettled by the epidemic of suicides that followed the "Anschluss"—the annexation of Austria into Nazi Germany in 1938—was similar. As Gay notes, "During the spring, some five hundred Austrian Jews chose to kill themselves to elude humiliation, unbearable anxiety, or deportation to concentration camps. The casualties were so conspicuous that in late March the authorities felt compelled to issue a denial of the 'rumours of thousands of suicides since the Nazi accession to power.'"[5] In this environment of virulent persecution of the Jews, and feeling momentarily hopeless about the chances of escape, Anna asked her father, "Wouldn't it be better if we all killed ourselves?" To which Freud acerbically replied, "Why? Because they would like us to?" Gay comments further:

> He might grumble that the game was not worth the candle and talk with longing for the curtain to fall, but he was not about to blow out the candle, or leave the stage, at the convenience of the enemy. The defiant mood that dominated so much of Freud's life was still stirring in him. If he had to go, he would go on his own conditions.[6]

And once again, a small story, which may be apocryphal, but if so, it is a myth worth retaining. Just before the Nazis finally let him leave for England, and following a long series of humiliating demands for certification, for money and the like, the Gestapo required him to sign another document. It read:

> I Prof Freud hereby confirm that after the Anschluss of Austria by the German Reich, I have been treated by the Austrian authorities and particularly by the Gestapo with all the respect and consideration due to my academic reputation, that I could live and work in full freedom, that I could continue to pursue my activities in every way I desired, that I found full support from all concerned in that respect, and that I have not the slightest reason for any complaint.

Freud duly signed this document, for what else could he do? But he added a sentence that has become famous both as an instance of his ingrained ironic powers, and perhaps also as evidence in support of his theory that we all harbor a drive toward death. "*Ich kann die Gestapo jedermann auf das beste empfehlen,*" he wrote: "I can most highly recommend the Gestapo to everyone." Mark Edmundson comments:

> There's brilliance, as well as remarkable daring, in Freud's send-off to the Nazis. He offered them a statement with a latent and a manifest content, with a double-meaning. And double meanings (and triple meanings and proliferating, complex meanings of all sorts) were precisely what Nazis were allergic to, what they had, in effect, constructed their world to shut out. To the Nazis, there always had to be one: one people, one nation, one leader, and one meaning, the truth. The Gestapo must have been most flattered by the old Professor's compliment.[7]

Gay's reading of this is more panicky, seeing it as deeply dangerous:

> Freud was lucky the SS men reading his recommendation did not perceive the heavy sarcasm lurking in it. Nothing would have been more natural than to find his words offensive. Why, then, at the moment of liberation, take such a deadly risk? Was there something at work in Freud making him want to stay, and die, in Vienna? Whatever the reason, his "praise" of the Gestapo was Freud's last act of defiance on Austrian soil.[8]

This act of defiance might also reflect the more psychoanalytic type of resistance that one can see in Freud in the 1930s. Clinically, resistance denotes the patient's ambivalence, whereby they might be genuinely seeking therapeutic help yet might also be undermining attempts to achieve insight into the unconscious source or meaning of the symptoms which have been causing trouble, hence subverting the therapeutic process. More to the point, resistance runs alongside other defenses against knowledge—denial in all its forms—in which the person concerned converts, to adapt the famous classification, "known knowns" into "unknown knowns," or sometimes "unknown unknowns." Freud, like a very substantial number of liberal and enlightened Europeans of his period, did not believe what he saw when the Nazis came to power. He thought the Nazi phenomenon would be short-lived, then he thought that the Austrians would never become as brutal as the Germans (as we know, this was the opposite of the truth), then that the Church would offer protection, and then the League of Nations and France and Britain. None of this happened and the only protective forces Freud could rely on, and these were real and effective, were outstandingly devoted friends who had access to wealth and power.

But the point here is not the failure of the forces of apparent reason to step in to stop the whirlwind; nor is it just simply to note that one potent factor in the Nazis' success was the failure of decent people to recognize what was happening or to believe just how outrageous and blatant evil of this kind could be. Rather, it is to recognize something strange about Freud himself. His work had shown just how powerful the forces of irrationality are, and just how "feeble" (his word about the ego) is the human capacity to counteract it. His great socio-psychological work of 1930, *Civilization and Its Discontents*, was devoted largely to uncovering the destructive power of the Death Drive—delineating in detail the powerlessness of the "civilized" world in which Freud and other Europeans believed to forestall the explosions of violence that could come at any time, with the smallest trigger.[9] These triggers were all around and very familiar to Freud: financial collapse, the appeal of authoritarianism, endemic and insurmountable antisemitism, and so on. Why should Freud have thought that anything other than death would happen in such dire circumstances? He may have been a stoic and ironist, but there is plenty of evidence that if the stakes were high enough and the anxiety too great, he could also, like his most naïve patient, avoid the truth.

It is worth noting that what was true for Freud was also true for some other analysts, particularly in Germany, who either saw the Nazis as a passing phenomenon or who thought that it was possible to deal with them. Historical work over the past forty years has shown clearly that German psychoanalysts followed a policy of "appeasement" toward the Nazis, characterized by an attempt to distance psychoanalysis from its "Jewish" elements.[10] Under the leadership of the non-Jewish analysts Felix Boehm and Carl Müller-Braunschweig, and with the support of Ernest Jones (then President of the International Psychoanalytical Association) and, to some extent, even of Freud and his daughter Anna, the attitude of the Germans was to try to preserve the psychoanalytic movement even if it meant compromising with the Nazis. This involved the forced resignation of the Jewish analysts from the German Psychoanalytic Society in 1935. It also sparked an intellectual effort to distance psychoanalysis from the Freudian focus on sexuality and the opposition between the unconscious and the social order, replacing it with the project of releasing the potential of the German unconscious in the service of the state. In 1936, the remaining psychoanalysts in Germany joined with other psychotherapists under the leadership of the Nazi psychiatrist Matthias Heinrich Göring to form the German Institute for Psychological Research and Psychotherapy—known, colloquially and lastingly, as the Göring Institute. By 1938, the Psychoanalytic Society had been dissolved, but its members continued as a "Work Group" within the Göring Institute, and some of them—including Boehm and Müller-Braunschweig—retained senior positions. Through their involvement with the Göring Institute, which had the privileged status of a "Reichsinstitute," they occupied an important place in the Nazi state, offering treatment to homosexuals and to war-traumatized members of the Luftwaffe, and participating in the construction of a "New German Psychotherapy" based, at least in name, on a non-Freudian and antisemitic ideology, and dedicated to the construction of model citizens of the Nazi Reich. Freud, therefore, was not the only one in denial. By 1938, in any case, his resistance to seeing what was going on had faded, although Freud was still reluctant to leave Austria. This resistance, however, was overcome by a trauma that even he could not avoid feeling to the core of his old bones.

The trauma was Anna's arrest by the Gestapo on March 22, 1938. Anna was the center of Freud's life by this point. As described previously, Freud had analyzed Anna in an act that would nowadays be seen as deeply unethical and compromising; and he appeared to have had guilt feelings over the likelihood that this experience had prevented her from ever leaving him and forming sexually intimate, loving relationships of her own. Not only was she now his nurse, changing his prosthesis and looking after him physically, but she was also his confidante, his representative, and the major loyalist among the new generation of psychoanalysts. She was the only one of his children to follow him in the field he had created, which she did with genuine distinction. By the 1930s, Freud was highly dependent on her, and she rose to the requirements of this dependency with enormous ability and great resolve. So when the Gestapo arrived at Berggasse 19, Freud's home, wanting to arrest Freud, ostensibly because they believed the International Psychoanalytical Association was a subversive organization, Anna went in his place (Marie Bonaparte, who was Princess of Greece and the leading psychoanalyst in France also volunteered, but the Gestapo would not allow her to go along). Worrying about what would be done to Anna, Max Schur, Freud's doctor, gave her enough of the barbital drug Veronal to kill herself if she needed to do so. It is not clear exactly what happened, only that Anna showed the presence of mind to ensure she was not left waiting to be interviewed, which might have meant she was simply taken off to a concentration camp at the end of the day like so many other

Jews abandoned in the corridors of Gestapo headquarters. Instead, she got herself interrogated relatively quickly and somehow persuaded her interviewers that the psychoanalytic organization was indeed a scientific one. Perhaps the fact that the American ambassador, as well as the Princess of Greece, were on Freud's case, and that President Roosevelt had given direct instructions to the American consulate to intervene if necessary, had some impact on the Nazis. Anna was released and allowed home, where her father had been pacing all day; according to Schur, this was one of the rare times when Freud showed deep emotion.

At this point, Freud gave in to those who wanted him to get out of Vienna and were willing to go to extraordinary lengths to make it possible for him to do so. Marie Bonaparte paid a big portion of the taxes that the Nazis imposed in their brilliantly vindictive bureaucratic way, taxes which first removed the assets of their victims and then demanded that they were paid for. Anna tirelessly worked her way around the formalities, the various forms (e.g., the *Unbedenklischkeitserklärung* or "statement of no impediment"), and attestations that had to be provided and paid for at every stage. Ernest Jones, Freud's most loyal follower, negotiated directly in Britain with the President of the Royal Society (who did not believe the Jews were really being harmed in Vienna) and through him with the Home Secretary, Sir Samuel Hoare. Fortunately, Jones and Hoare had what author David Cohen calls an "unlikely bond": "the two men had gone figure skating together; it should be remembered that before he wrote his biography of Freud, Jones' most successful book was *The Elements of Figure Skating*."[11] Even the Nazi in control of Freud's affairs, Anton Sauerwald, unaccountably helped get the necessary agreement to ship Freud's possessions to England, an unexpected luxury that meant more to Freud than we might realize, as he eventually succeeded in recreating his home in what is now the Freud Museum in Hampstead. Freud finally left on June 4, 1938, accompanied by his wife Martha, Anna, a substitute for his doctor, who had appendicitis, his housemaid Paula Fichtl, and his beloved chow, Lün. Several other members of the family were included on the list of those given permits to leave with Freud, and they went out in the surrounding period, to reconvene in London. Freud's four elderly sisters remained behind, too weak, it seems, to leave Vienna; and they all died in the Holocaust.

Freud traveled first to Paris, where Marie Bonaparte gave him a perfect day of solace and care in her home, and then on to England, arriving at Victoria Station on the morning of June 6, 1938, to a kind of celebrity welcome and genuine warmth that touched the old man deeply, and is to England's everlasting credit. There was much that was hard: he had to live in temporary accommodation for a while; he was worried about his sisters; he could not go up the stairs to visit his beloved sister-in-law Minna, who was terminally ill and bedridden; his cancer was progressing, and soon he would face yet more terrible operations on his jaw; and his dog was in quarantine. Incidentally, he visited the dog, but he persuaded the secretary of the Royal Society to bring their book to him for signature, because he was ostensibly too sick to go out. This gesture on the part of the Royal Society was deeply touching: the only previous time the Charter Book had been taken out of the Society was for the King of England. Letters flooded in from all and sundry, many of them simply from well-wishers pleased that he had survived and that England was showing him hospitality. Gay writes:

> Famous personages and ordinary Englishmen, total strangers nearly all of them, gave Freud a reception genial and thoughtful almost beyond his capacity for acceptance. "We have become popular all of a sudden," he wrote [Max] Eitingon. "The manager in the bank says, 'I know all about you'; the chauffeur driving Anna observes, 'Oh, it's Dr Freud's place.' We are choking in flowers."[12]

To his brother, Alexander, who had left Austria for Switzerland in March, Freud wrote,

> England is "a blessed, a happy land, inhabited by kindly, hospitable people ... " He was amazed to see that from the third day of his stay, letters bearing only such addresses as "Dr Freud, London" or "Overlooking Regent's Park" had reached him.[13]

And apart from letters from those wishing to convert him to Christianity, most of the reception was genuine and generous in a way that even Freud, a great cynic, could appreciate.

Death and Legacy

The story of Freud's final year of life is one of outward peace followed by final decline, terrible sickness—so bad that his beloved dog would not come near him because of the smell from his jaw—and a dignified death, what would now be called an assisted suicide at the hands of Max Schur, with Anna's agreement and possibly her help. As others have pointed out, the manner of this death was important: the old realist, suffering and unable to work, saying to his doctor, "Schur, you remember our 'contract' not to leave me in the lurch when the time had come. Now it is nothing but torture and makes no sense."[14] Helped by Schur's morphine, he died on September 23, 1939, which, no doubt coincidentally, was the solemn Jewish day of facing up to oneself, Yom Kippur (the Day of Atonement). Later, Anna Freud would become one of the world's most important psychoanalysts; and in the war years, there would be a split in the British Psychoanalytic Society caused by the antagonism between her and the other major psychoanalytic "daughter" of Freud in Britain, Melanie Klein, a split which has still not been fully resolved. But at this time, there was a genuine sense of an old era that had gone its way, the truths and limits of psychoanalysis coming to the fore. Freud's faith in the advancement of reason and science would have to give way to the demonstration of the deeper truth that psychoanalysis displays: that we are enemies to ourselves, and that our destructiveness knows very little limit.

Let us go back momentarily to Freud's late style. Throughout the 1930s, he worked along two main lines: bringing the technical theory of psychoanalysis up to date (e.g., the *New Introductory Lectures*; *Analysis Terminable and Interminable*) and the "historical fantasy," *Moses and Monotheism*. The technical works are of great importance and show a mind still working with phenomenal clarity and synthetic power. But *Moses and Monotheism* is a special, more personal work. In many ways, it was the culmination of Freud's other important "social" works written in the 1920s, notably *The Future of an Illusion*, which was his account of religion, and *Civilization and Its Discontents*, in which he explored what he saw as the unremitting tension between the desires of the individual, rooted in their unconscious impulses, and the necessity for control of these by society. For Freud, the development of social structures is due primarily to individuals' need for protection. Fearful of the forces of nature, of the weakness of the body and of the actions of other people, individuals form together in groups to defend themselves. These groups become what Freud termed "civilization," defined as "the whole sum of the achievements and the regulations which distinguish our lives from those of our animal ancestors and which serve two purposes—namely to protect men against nature and to adjust their mutual relations."[15] However, just as psychological defenses can cause problems even while they protect the ego against the ravages of unconscious life, so is civilization a compromise between the need of people to live together and the fundamentally asocial demands of the unconscious. This means that people always have to give up something for the sake of social survival. In this sense, society is opposed to the individual, even though it is also essential to life. Civilization is a necessary evil that always brings unhappiness.

The Future of an Illusion presented religion as an "illusion" whereby the pains of life are ameliorated. The details of this concept are revealing in that they show how devoted an adherent Freud was to a "rationalist" perspective that refused any mystical consolations or illusions. For Freud, religion is precisely such an illusion, built on infantile dependence—the need for protection and the wish that it will be offered by a powerful, superior being who has sought us out. Freud recognized the appeal of this but was also certain that it was time for religious illusions to be overcome and that by blocking a true understanding of reality they were doing great damage. "Surely infantilism is destined to be surmounted," he writes in the book. "Men cannot remain children for ever; they must in the end go out into 'hostile life.' We may call this 'education to reality.'"[16] The task of psychoanalysis in exposing the roots of religion is parallel to its task when faced with neurotic patients. Just as a patient's symptoms will have developed for good reason, to protect the ego against what might seem to be something worse, a society's symptoms, including the development of religion, will have defensive functions. But these defenses tend to turn destructive, which is what turns them into neurotic symptoms. They cause too much further unhappiness, and they need to be outgrown.

Moses and Monotheism seems to develop out of these two books as well as the earlier *Totem and Taboo*, but it can also be persuasively read as an expression of Freud's personal identity crisis, or at least quandary over his Jewish identity in the 1930s. This reading is legitimized in part by his own successive "prefaces" to the book, as he worried about the propriety of publishing it. In the beginning, Freud set this context of anxiety as relating to the Jewish people and his possible betrayal of them in a time of trouble; significantly, he did not hesitate to remind the reader of his own membership of this disparaged group.

> To deprive a people of a man whom they take pride in as the greatest of their sons is not a thing to be gladly or carelessly undertaken, least of all by someone who is himself one of them.[17]

Freud's defense of his actions, as ever, was in the name of scientific truth, reflecting his deep-rooted if increasingly pessimistic belief that the only viable route to human progress is through the dispelling of illusions and the exercise of rationality.

> But we cannot allow any such reflection to induce us to put the truth aside in favor of what are supposed to be national interests; and, moreover, the clarification of a set of facts may be expected to bring us a gain in knowledge.[18]

In Freud's universe, nothing, even the maintenance of Jewish self-esteem, was more important than a "gain in knowledge." However, Freud's main cautions about publication were not caused by worry over its effect on the Jews, but by fear that it would incite the wrath of external authorities on psychoanalysis itself. This is clearest in his "Prefatory Note" to the third part of the book, written in Vienna before the Anschluss of March 1938. Here, Freud expresses anxiety about alienating the Catholic authorities when they might be the only protection against the "prehistoric barbarism" of Nazism—a hope demonstrating that Freud's reading of political events was not as perspicacious as his reading of psychology. Even while holding onto this hope, however, Freud was characteristically ironic and negative in his framing: the old power is to be invested in only because it is less destructive than the new. "The new enemy," he notes acerbically, "to whom we want to avoid being of service, is more dangerous than the old one with which we have already learned to come to terms."[19] Psychoanalysis, Freud rather proudly claims, will always draw "the resentment of our ruling powers down upon us" because it "reduces religion to a neurosis of humanity," so there is not really much chance of finding protection in the Church.[20] However, where there is little hope, what there is must be preserved, so Freud, uncertain of the impact of his book, chose to withhold it from publication, clinging to the idea that in so doing he might be helping psychoanalysis retain its home. "Psychoanalysis," he wrote, in terms resonant of his state of mind, "which in the course of my long life has gone everywhere, still possesses no home that could be more valuable for it than the city in which it was born and grew up."[21]

A few months later, however, Vienna's and Freud's circumstances had changed: the former was in Nazi hands, the latter in England. As part of a further "Prefatory Note," Freud wrote: "In the certainty that I should now be persecuted not only for my line of thought but also for my 'race'—accompanied by many of my friends, I left the city which, from my early childhood, had been my home for seventy-eight years."[22] External causes for delaying publication were no longer there. England had proved friendly, if rather prone to be a source of Christian attempts to save Freud's poor soul, and there was nothing anymore to be hoped for by way of protection for psychoanalysis from the "broken reed" of Austrian Catholicism. The uncertainties now were only internal, Freud's "lack of the consciousness of unity and belonging together which should exist between an author and his work," his "critical sense" that "this book, which takes its start from the man Moses, appears like a dancer balancing on the tip of one toe."[23] But time and energy had run out, and the deep investment Freud had in this final great work was such that he could not hold it back from its readership. Indeed, thinking psychoanalytically as we must about Freud's work, the very existence of all the uncertainties and anxieties, the breaches with logic and narrative sense, the "lack of balance" and anxiety that this generated, all suggest that there were powerful emotional identifications and wishes at work. It is not hard to see what these might have been. The identification was clearly with Moses, the one who—like Freud—brought a benighted people out into the light of order and law; the wish was that psychoanalysis, like Judaism, might survive its dispersal.

Thus, at the very end of his life, ready "to die in freedom," Freud let loose on the world his meditation on the origins of Judaism, and on the perseverance of Jewish identity. The historian of Judaism Yosef Hayim Yerushalmi offers a comprehensive account of what *Moses and Monotheism* might be about.

> If the book can be read as the final chapter in Freud's lifelong case history, it is also a public statement about matters of considerably wider consequence—the nature of Jewish history, religion and peoplehood, Christianity and anti-Semitism—written at a tragic historical juncture.[24]

In particular, Yerushalmi argues that "the true axis of the book" is "the problem of tradition"—the question of what perpetuates the past and, specifically, gives Judaism its continued hold over Jews, even those who, like Freud, did not have a trace of religious belief in them.[25]

Moses and Monotheism can be seen as a record of Freud's emotional response to Nazism and his attempt to work out his relationship with his Jewish identity in that context. It is also an exploration of the conditions that have allowed the survival and reproduction of Judaism in a hostile environment. Hence it deals, as Yerushalmi claims, with questions of tradition and inheritance, as well as opening out domains of speculation on national and political identity, the aspect of the book that Said draws out. It is thus a moving and complex document at numerous personal and intellectual levels. Freud also gives a startling account of antisemitism that embodies some of the recurrent themes of psychoanalysis' encounter with otherness, perhaps particularly in terms of its own institutional history. This account focuses on how the Jew represents elements in the antisemite's psychic constitution that are uncomfortable or threatening, and are consequently repudiated, yet are also objects of fascination. Because of the history of Christian antisemitism, which laid the important mythological groundwork for the pervasiveness of antisemitic beliefs in Western culture, the Jew is the chosen carrier of these unwanted yet seductive projections. In addition, there are real attributes of Jews and Judaism (such as circumcision, monotheism, and the idea of the "chosen people") that help fuel this set of compelling myths.

In the limited bibliography of psychoanalytic studies of antisemitism, this generally Freudian account has continued to hold sway. How this has happened and what it means now is a complex story. But we cannot get away from the fact that, exiled from and ridiculed in his homeland, welcomed as he was into a new land that had only a vague inkling of his teachings and that had itself plenty of ambivalence toward its Jewish citizens, Freud chose to aggressively follow a line of thinking that makes Jewish identity problematic, and to assert the superiority of Judaism over other religions and the envy to which that makes its adherents prone. There is nothing quiet and accepting about this. He may have wanted to die in freedom, but he was clear that he was not willing to just fade away.

Notes

Preface

1 Auden, W. (1940) In Memory of Sigmund Freud. In W. Auden, *Collected Shorter Poems 1927–1957*. London: Faber (1966), p.168.
2 Gay, P. (1988) *Freud: A Life for Our Time*. London: Dent, p. 588.
3 *Newsweek*, March 27, 2006.

Chapter 1

1 Wordsworth, W. (1802) My Heart Leaps Up. In H. Gardner (ed) (1972) *The New Oxford Book of English Verse*. Oxford: Clarenden Press, p.502.
2 Freud, S. (1900) The Interpretation of Dreams. *The Standard Edition of the Complete Psychological Works of Sigmund Freud, Volume IV (1900): The Interpretation of Dreams*. London: Hogarth Press.
3 Freud, The Interpretation of Dreams, pp.210–11.
4 Ibid., p.215.
5 Ibid., pp.216–17.
6 Ibid., p.xxvi (Preface to the Second Edition, 1908).
7 Freud, S. (1925) An Autobiographical Study. *The Standard Edition of the Complete Psychological Works of Sigmund Freud, Volume XX (1925–1926): An Autobiographical Study, Inhibitions, Symptoms and Anxiety, The Question of Lay Analysis and Other Works*. London: Hogarth Press, pp.7–8.
8 Gilman, S. (1993) *Freud, Race and Gender*. Princeton, NJ: Princeton University Press, p.14.
9 Freud, An Autobiographical Study, p.8.
10 Freud, The Interpretation of Dreams, p.194.
11 Klein, D. (1985) *Jewish Origins of the Psychoanalytic Movement*. Chicago, IL: Chicago University Press, p.42.
12 Makari, G. (2008) *Revolution in Mind*. London: Duckworth, p.21.

13 Gallo, R. (2010) *Freud's Mexico*. Cambridge, MA: MIT Press.
14 Freud, The Interpretation of Dreams, p.196.
15 Ibid., p.197.
16 Boyarin, D. (1997) *Unheroic Conduct*. Berkeley: University of California Press.
17 Freud, The Interpretation of Dreams, p.138.
18 Ibid., p.483.
19 Roudinesco, E. (2016) *Freud in His Time and Ours*. Cambridge, MA: Harvard University Press, p.15.
20 Ibid., p.17.
21 Ibid.
22 Gay, P. (1988) *Freud: A Life for Our Time*. London: Dent, p.14.
23 Freud, An Autobiographical Study, p.8.
24 Ibid.
25 Jacoby, R. (1983) *The Repression of Psychoanalysis*. New York: Basic Books, p.124.

Chapter 2

1 Makari, *Revolution in Mind*, p.23.
2 Ibid., p.24.
3 Roudinesco, *Freud in His Time and Ours*, p.34.
4 Freud, S. (1882) Letter from Sigmund Freud to Martha Bernays, June 19, 1882. In E. L. Freud (ed) (1961) *Letters of Sigmund Freud 1873–1939*. London: Hogarth Press, pp.7–8.
5 Roudinesco, *Freud in His Time and Ours*, p.50.
6 Freud, S. (1882) Letter from Sigmund Freud to Martha Bernays, July 23, 1882. In E. L. Freud, *Letters of Sigmund Freud 1873–1939*, pp.21–2.
7 Makari, *Revolution in Mind*, p.26.
8 Freud, S. (1885) Letter from Sigmund Freud to Martha Bernays, November 24, 1885. In E. L. Freud, *Letters of Sigmund Freud 1873–1939*, p.184.

9 Breuer, J. (1893) Fräulein Anna O, Case Histories from Studies on Hysteria. *The Standard Edition of the Complete Psychological Works of Sigmund Freud, Volume II (1893–1895): Studies on Hysteria*. London: Hogarth Press, p.24.

10 Ibid., p.26.

11 Ibid., p.30.

12 Jones, E. (1957) *Sigmund Freud Life and Work, Volume One: The Young Freud 1856–1900*. London: Hogarth Press, p.247.

13 Breuer, J. and Freud, S. (1893) On The Psychical Mechanism of Hysterical Phenomena. *The Standard Edition of the Complete Psychological Works of Sigmund Freud, Volume II (1893–1895): Studies on Hysteria*. London: Hogarth Press, p.7.

14 Freud, S. (1893) The Psychotherapy of Hysteria from *Studies on Hysteria. The Standard Edition of the Complete Psychological Works of Sigmund Freud Volume II (1893–1895): Studies on Hysteria*. London: Hogarth Press, p.305.

15 Gay, *Freud: A Life for Our Time*, p.67.

16 Makari, *Revolution in Mind*, p.72.

17 Gay, *Freud: A Life for Our Time*, p.78.

18 Freud, S. (1896) Letter from Freud to Fliess, May 4, 1896. In J. Masson (ed) *The Complete Letters of Sigmund Freud to Wilhelm Fliess, 1887–1904*. Cambridge, MA: Belknap Press (1986), p.186.

Chapter 3

1 Breuer, J. and Freud, S. (1895) Studies on Hysteria. *The Standard Edition of the Complete Psychological Works of Sigmund Freud Volume II(1893–1895): Studies on Hysteria*. London: Hogarth Press.

2 Freud, The Interpretation of Dreams, p.xxvi.

3 Whitebook, J. (2017) *Freud: An Intellectual Biography*. Cambridge: Cambridge University Press, pp.219–20.

4 Knoepfmacher, H. (1979) Sigmund Freud and the B'Nai B'Rith. *Journal of the American Psychoanalytic Association*, 27, 441–9, pp.442–3.
5 Diller, J. (1991) *Freud's Jewish Identity: A Case Study in the Impact of Ethnicity*. London: Associated University Presses, p.22.
6 Klein, *Jewish Origins of the Psychoanalytic Movement*, p.74.
7 Freud, S. (1926) Letter from Sigmund Freud to Members of The B'nai B'rith Lodge, May 6, 1926. In E. L. Freud, *Letters of Sigmund Freud 1873–1939*, p.366.
8 Ibid., pp.366–7.
9 Freud, The Interpretation of Dreams, p.214.
10 Ibid., p.173.
11 Ibid., p.434.
12 Anzieu, D. (1975). *Freud's Self-Analysis*. London: Hogarth Press, p.200.
13 Freud, The Interpretation of Dreams, p.121.
14 Roudinesco, *Freud in His Time and Ours*, p.446, n.57.
15 Freud, The Interpretation of Dreams, p.106.
16 Ibid., p.107.
17 Ibid., pp.118–19.
18 Ibid., pp.119–20.
19 Ibid., p.109.
20 Ibid., p.113.
21 Ibid., p.117.
22 Freud, S. (1905) Fragment of an Analysis of a Case of Hysteria. *The Standard Edition of the Complete Psychological Works of Sigmund Freud, Volume VII (1901–1905): A Case of Hysteria, Three Essays on Sexuality and Other Works*. London: Hogarth Press, pp.1–122.
23 Marcus, S. (1975) Freud and Dora: Story, History, Case History. In C. Bernheimer and C. Kahane (eds) *In Dora's Case*. London: Virago, pp.56–91.
24 Freud, S. (1901) The Psychopathology of Everyday Life. *The Standard Edition of the Complete Psychological Works of Sigmund Freud, Volume VI (1901): The Psychopathology of Everyday Life*. London: Hogarth Press, p.241.
25 Freud, Fragment of an Analysis of a Case of Hysteria, p.64.

26 Ibid., p.77.
27 Ibid.
28 Roudinesco, *Freud in His Time and Ours*, p.85.
29 Deutsch, F. (1957) A Footnote to Freud's "Fragment of an Analysis of a Case of Hysteria." *Psychoanalytic Quarterly*, 26, 159–67, p.167.

Chapter 4

1 Roudinesco, *Freud in His Time and Ours*, p. 236; Maciejewski, F. (2006) Freud, His Wife, and His "Wife". *American Imago*, 63, 497–506.
2 Makari, *Revolution in Mind*, p.90.
3 Ibid., p. 98.
4 Freud, S. (1897) Letter from Freud to Fliess, September 21, 1897. In J. Masson (ed) *The Complete Letters of Sigmund Freud to Wilhelm Fliess*. Cambridge, MA: Belknap Press (1986), p.264.
5 Ibid., p.266.
6 Roudinesco, *Freud in His Time and Ours*, p.74.
7 Freud, S. (1920) Beyond the Pleasure Principle. *The Standard Edition of the Complete Psychological Works of Sigmund Freud, Volume XVIII (1920–1922): Beyond the Pleasure Principle, Group Psychology and Other Work*. London: Hogarth Press, p.51.
8 Makari, *Revolution in Mind*, p.110.
9 Freud, S. (1905) Three Essays on the Theory of Sexuality. *The Standard Edition of the Complete Psychological Works of Sigmund Freud, Volume VII (1901–1905): A Case of Hysteria, Three Essays on Sexuality and Other Works*. London: Hogarth Press, p.231.
10 Ibid.
11 Marcus, Freud and Dora, p.79.
12 Freud, S. (1897) Letter 71 Extracts from the Fliess Papers. *The Standard Edition of the Complete Psychological Works of Sigmund Freud I*, 263–6. London: Hogarth Press, p.265.
13 Ibid.
14 Freud, S. (1933) New Introductory Lectures on Psycho-Analysis. *The Standard Edition of the Complete Psychological Works of Sigmund*

Freud, Volume XXII (1932–1936): New Introductory Lectures on Psycho-Analysis and Other Works. London: Hogarth Press, p.135.

15 Ibid., p.118.

16 Ibid., p.128.

17 Mitchell, J. (1974) *Psychoanalysis and Feminism*. Harmondsworth: Penguin.

18 Freud, *Three Essays on the Theory of Sexuality*, footnote (1915) to p.144.

Chapter 5

1 Roudinesco, *Freud in His Time and Ours*, p.115.

2 Makari, *Revolution in Mind*, p.154.

3 Stekel, W. (1926) On the History of the Analytical Movement. *Psychoanalysis and History*, 7, 99–130 (2005), p.102.

4 Svevo, I. (1923) *Zeno's Conscience*. Harmondsworth: Penguin.

5 Stekel, On the History of the Analytical Movement, p.104.

6 Gay, *Freud: A Life for Our Time*, p.419.

7 Freud, S. (1922) Letter from Freud to Lou Andreas-Salomé, March 13, 1922. *The International Psycho-Analytical Library*. New York: WW Norton (1985), 89, 113–4, p.113.

8 Gay, *Freud: A Life for Our Time*, p.58.

9 Roudinesco, *Freud in His Time and Ours*, p.116.

10 Freud, S. (1919) "A Child Is Being Beaten" A Contribution to the Study of the Origin of Sexual Perversions. *The Standard Edition of the Complete Psychological Works of Sigmund Freud Volume XVII*. London: Hogarth Press, pp.175–204.

11 Bair, D. (2004) *Jung: A Biography*. London: Little, Brown, p.166.

12 Grosskurth, P. (1985) *Melanie Klein*. London: Maresfield, p.159.

13 Makari, *Revolution in Mind*, p.217.

14 Freud, S. (1909) Notes Upon a Case of Obsessional Neurosis. *The Standard Edition of the Complete Psychological Works of Sigmund Freud X*. London: Hogarth Press, pp.151–318.

15 Maddox, B. (2006) *Freud's Wizard: The Enigma of Ernest Jones*. London: John Murray, p.3.
16 McGuire, W. (1974) *The Freud/Jung Letters*. Harmondsworth: Penguin, pp.133, 144.
17 Ibid., p.43.
18 Ibid., p.51.
19 Makari, *Revolution in Mind*, p.203.
20 Whitebook, *Freud: An Intellectual Biography*, p.262.
21 McGuire, *The Freud/Jung Letters*, p.56.
22 Freud, S. (1908) Letter from Sigmund Freud to Karl Abraham, May 3, 1908. In E. Falzeder (ed) (2002) *The Complete Correspondence of Sigmund Freud and Karl Abraham 1907–1925*. London: Routledge, p.38.
23 McGuire, *The Freud/Jung Letters*, pp.151–2.
24 Ibid., p.152.
25 Editors' Introduction to Freud, S. (1910). Five Lectures on Psycho-analysis. *The Standard Edition of the Complete Psychological Works of Sigmund Freud, Volume XI (1910): Five Lectures on Psycho-Analysis, Leonardo da Vinci and Other Works*. London: Hogarth Press, p.3.
26 McGuire, *The Freud/Jung Letters*, p.291.
27 Ibid., p.292.
28 Ibid.
29 Ibid., p.295.
30 Ibid., p.297.

Chapter 6

1 Freud, The Psychotherapy of Hysteria, p.305.
2 Freud, S. (1916–17) Introductory Lectures on Psycho-Analysis. *The Standard Edition of the Complete Psychological Works of Sigmund Freud, Volume XV and XVI*. London: Hogarth Press.
3 Freud, New Introductory Lectures on Psycho-Analysis, p.5.

4 Ibid.

5 Roudinesco, *Freud in His Time and Ours*, p.174.

6 Freud, S. (1914) On Narcissism: An Introduction. *The Standard Edition of the Complete Psychological Works of Sigmund Freud, Volume XIV (1914–1916): On the History of the Psycho-Analytic Movement, Papers on Metapsychology and Other Works*. London: Hogarth Press, pp.67–102.

7 Freud, S. (1917) Mourning and Melancholia. *The Standard Edition of the Complete Psychological Works of Sigmund Freud, Volume XIV (1914–1916): On the History of the Psycho-Analytic Movement, Papers on Metapsychology and Other Works*. London: Hogarth Press, pp.237–58.

8 Freud, Mourning and Melancholia, p.243.

9 Ibid., p.244.

10 Freud, Beyond the Pleasure Principle, p.53.

11 Ibid., p.38.

12 Ibid.

13 Ibid., p.15.

14 Ibid., p.16.

15 Freud, S. (1920) Letter from Sigmund Freud to Oskar Pfister, January 27, 1920. In E. L. Freud, *Letters of Sigmund Freud 1873–1939*, p.327.

16 Freud, S. (1920) Letter from Sigmund Freud to Sándor Ferenczi, January 29, 1920. In E. Brabant, E. Falzeder and P. Giampieri-Deutsch (eds) (1993) *The Correspondence of Sigmund Freud and Sándor Ferenczi, Volume 3, 1920–1933*. Cambridge: Harvard, p.6.

17 Gay, *Freud: A Life for Our Time*, p.392.

18 Ibid.

19 Freud, S. (1923) Letter from Sigmund Freud to Kata and Lajos Levy, June 11, 1923. In E. L. Freud, *Letters of Sigmund Freud 1873–1939*, p.344.

20 Freud, S. (1926) Letter from Freud to Ludwig Binswanger, October 15, 1926. In G. Fichner (ed) (2003) *The Sigmund Freud-Ludwig Binswanger Correspondence 1908–1938*. London: Open Gate Press, p.184.

21 Benveniste, D. (2015) *The Interwoven Lives of Sigmund, Anna and W. Ernest Freud*. New York: International Psychoanalytic Books.

22 Roudinesco, *Freud in His Time and Ours*, p.255.

23 Freud, A. (1923) The Relation of Beating-Phantasies to a Day-Dream. *International Journal of Psychoanalysis*, 4, 89–102.
24 Freud, Beyond the Pleasure Principle, pp.51–2.
25 Freud, S. (1923) The Ego and the Id. *The Standard Edition of the Complete Psychological Works of Sigmund Freud, Volume XIX (1923–1925): The Ego and the Id and Other Works*. London: Hogarth Press, p.23.
26 Ibid., p.29.

Chapter 7

1 Freud, S. (1928) Letter from Sigmund Freud to Sándor Ferenczi, October 12, 1928. In E. L. Freud, *Letters of Sigmund Freud 1873–1939*, p.382.
2 Freud, S. (1939) Moses and Monotheism. *The Standard Edition of the Complete Psychological Works of Sigmund Freud, Volume XXIII (1937–1939): Moses and Monotheism, An Outline of Psycho-Analysis and Other Works*. London: Hogarth Press, pp.1–138.
3 Said, E. (2003) *Freud and the Non-European*. London: Verso, p.29.
4 Gay, *Freud: A Life for Our Time*, p.626.
5 Ibid., pp.621–2.
6 Ibid., p.622.
7 Edmundson, M. (2007) *The Death of Sigmund Freud*. London: Bloomsbury, p.122.
8 Gay, *Freud: A Life for Our Time*, p.628.
9 Freud, S. (1930) Civilization and Its Discontents. *The Standard Edition of the Complete Psychological Works of Sigmund Freud, Volume XXI (1927–1931): The Future of an Illusion, Civilization and Its Discontents, and Other Works*. London: Hogarth Press, pp.57–146.
10 Frosh, S. (2005) *Hate and the Jewish Science: Nazism, Antisemitism and Psychoanalysis*. London: Palgrave.
11 Cohen, D. (2010) *The Escape of Sigmund Freud*. London: JR Books, p.153.
12 Gay, *Freud: A Life for Our Time*, p.631.

13 Ibid.

14 Ibid., p.651.

15 Freud, Civilization and Its Discontents, p.89.

16 Freud, S. (1927) The Future of an Illusion. *The Standard Edition of the Complete Psychological Works of Sigmund Freud, Volume XXI (1927–1931): The Future of an Illusion, Civilization and Its Discontents, and Other Works*. London: Hogarth Press, p.49.

17 Freud, Moses and Monotheism, p.7.

18 Ibid.

19 Ibid., p.55.

20 Ibid.

21 Ibid.

22 Ibid., p.57.

23 Ibid., p.58.

24 Yerushalmi, Y. (1991) *Freud's Moses*. New Haven, CT: Yale University Press, p.2.

25 Ibid., p.29.

Suggested Reading

There is an enormous literature on Freud, who continues to fascinate writers and readers even though so many of his theories remain controversial. The first important biography was written by Ernest Jones, whose *Sigmund Freud: Life and Work* was published in three volumes between 1953 and 1957. This book is also available in a shortened, one-volume edition published by Penguin. It remains an indispensable resource, as Jones was a close follower and friend of Freud, serving as president of both the International Psychoanalytic Association and the British Psychoanalytical Society in their formative years (he founded the latter). He was very well versed in the history of psychoanalysis and participated in much of it, and he also had the trust of Anna Freud when writing the book. On the other hand, not only is this biography now old and so could not take recent scholarship into account, but it is also very much an "official" view of Freud, with most potential criticisms and problems ignored or set aside. That said, it gives a tremendously rounded sense of Freud as a person and offers a powerful evocation of his time.

Among later biographies, there are at least two of real stature. Peter Gay's (1988) *Freud: A Life for Our Time* is comprehensive, very well written, and manages to combine a deeply felt account of Freud's life with a very clear guide to his ideas. Gay was an outstanding historian and a convert to psychoanalysis, and he brought these two features together in an illuminating way. Like Jones's book, it is rather short on criticism of Freud, but this is more than made up for by the richness of the characterization. More recently, Elisabeth Roudinesco, who is very well known in Europe for her work on French psychoanalysis, has taken advantage of the opening of the Freud archives in the Library of Congress to produce a rich, quirky, opinionated, and powerful new biography called *Freud in His Time and Ours*, a title that echoes Gay's from an earlier generation. This is an excellent book and a very readable one, and despite Roudinesco's strong views, it is quite well balanced. It was published in English in 2016.

A recent alternative biography is Joel Whitebook's (2017) *Freud: An Intellectual Biography*. It is another big book, but focuses on Freud's theories and on some of his most important relationships, especially those with Wilhelm Fliess and Carl Jung. It is not as biographically informative as Roudinesco's book, but it offers an interesting account of Freud's relative reluctance to explore issues in his relationship with his mother, and of how this might have affected his ideas. Adam Phillips's (2014) *Becoming Freud: The Making of a Psychoanalyst* is another idiosyncratic book reflecting this thoughtful British psychotherapist's lifelong engagement with Freud as a humanist and writer.

Then there is Freud himself. He was a wonderful writer in German and, on the whole, this is reflected in English translations, even if they rarely manage to convey his exact tone and expressive nuance. The Standard Edition of Freud's works appeared over a considerable period of time under the general editorship of James Strachey and suffers from a tendency to make Freud more scientific and technical than he usually was in German—for example, by translating the German terms for "I" and "it" into "ego" and "id," or by using the obscure word "cathexis" when "investment" might have been just as effective. Nevertheless, the Standard Edition is a great scholarly achievement, and it is through this text that awareness of Freud and of his terminology has entered the English-speaking culture. The more recent translations published by Penguin are on the whole more literary in feel, though there is a bit of frustration with them because of wide variations in terminology and style between different volumes. In 2024, the South African psychoanalyst Mark Solms produced an "official" revision of the Standard Edition which is based on the Strachey original whilst including much recent scholarship as well as several essays that were excluded from the earlier work. This will undoubtedly be the standard way of reading Freud in English for some time.

Which of Freud's works to read? I recommend the *Introductory Lectures in Psychoanalysis*, and the *Five Lectures on Psychoanalysis*, both of which are brilliantly clear expositions of Freud's thought derived from live presentations and maintaining the sense of his presence as a speaker. *The Interpretation of Dreams*, the major *Case Histories* ("Dora," "Little Hans," the "Rat Man," and the "Wolf Man") all remain fantastically good reads, even if the technical sections of some of them are hard going. Freud's book *Jokes and Their Relation to the Unconscious* is rather too full of ancient Jewish misogynistic jokes for many modern tastes, but on the other hand, it is witty and interesting in part. *The Psychopathology of Everyday Life*, with its cataloging of bungled actions, slips of tongue and memory, and other kinds of motivated mistakes, is fascinating and at times hilarious. It is really worth reading Freud, even if not everything he wrote stands up to scrutiny. For readers who have access to university libraries, the online resource *Psychoanalytic Electronic Publishing* carries the complete works of Freud, as well as all major psychoanalytic publications from the past 130 years.

Finally, there are many introductions to psychoanalysis that do not stop at Freud. I will restrict myself to recommending one by my colleague Daniel Pick, *Psychoanalysis: A Very Short Introduction*, which is genuinely very short but packed full of insights and information; and my own *Brief Introduction to Psychoanalytic Theory*, which is not really so brief, but offers an overview of many important Freudian and post-Freudian ideas.

Index